MW00534713

# THE COMPLETE GUIDE TO ROTTWEILERS

Vanessa Richie

Publication Data

Vanessa Richie

The Complete Guide to Rottweilers ---- First edition.

Summary: "Successfully raising a Rottweiler dog from puppy to old age" --- Provided by publisher.

ISBN: 978-1-70433-3-038

[1. Rottweilers --- Non-Fiction] I. Title.

This book has been written with the published intent to provide accurate and author-itative information in regard to the subject matter included. While every reasonable pre-caution has been taken in preparation of this book the author and publisher expressly dis-claim responsibility for any errors, omissions, or adverse effects arising from the use or application of the information contained inside. The techniques and suggestions are to be used at the reader's discretion and are not to be considered a substitute for professional veterinary care. If you suspect a medical problem with your dog, consult your veterinarian.

Design by Sorin Rădulescu

First paperback edition, 2019

# TABLE OF CONTENTS

# INTRODUCTION

When anyone mentions the Rottweiler, a definite image comes to mind. However, from their sleek black coats to their reputation as guard dogs, what you imagine is probably only half accurate. Rottweilers, often called Rotties within the breed community, are one of the most loving and affectionate dogs among the large breeds. While they are definitely protective, anyone who has had a Rottie knows just how playful and affectionate they can be. If you let them, these massive dogs will try to turn your lap into their pillow of choice. Contrary to their formidable reputation and intimidating appearance, the Rottweilers' gentle nature and intelligence made them the first breed to be used as guide dogs.

Rottweilers' appearance is unmistakable. Their short black coats are easy to manage and give them a very distinctive look. The brown to rust-colored markings that appear on their face, chest, and legs tend to add a bit of charm and take away from their otherwise fierce appearance. This is a dog that, full grown, starts at around 80 pounds and caps at around 135 pounds, so it is definitely a large breed. At their best, Rottweilers have a lot of muscle; if you aren't careful, though, they do have a tendency to overeat, making obesity a problem you will need to avoid in order to keep your Rottie happy and healthy.

A combination of intelligence and a desire to please their owner makes Rotties one of the easiest large breeds to train, but you definitely have to establish your role as the leader. Your Rottie will have to learn to look to you for instructions to restrain his natural desire to protect you and your family.

This is not a breed for first-time dog owners because they have an extensive history as working dogs. Because of their high energy levels, daily exercise is required, even if you have a yard, and daily or frequent training sessions are best over the course of a Rottie's life because of their intellect. If not properly socialized, Rotties can be dangerous. Properly socialized Rotties, though, can be one of the best family dogs because of how loyal, confident, and playful they are.

The Rottweiler is a fantastic family dog, although you will need to be careful around small children. Given their size and general enthusiasm for play, young Rotties may not understand that it is incredibly easy to knock over a small child. However, that desire to protect them from others will be equally strong, so if you keep your dog calm, you really could not ask for a better protector. If you already have dogs, it is best to start with a puppy, unless you know that the adult Rottie you want to purchase or adopt is well socialized.

CHAPTER 1.
# Breed History And Characteristics

*"The Rottweiler has a lot of strong characteristics, and this breed isn't for everybody. They are strong and most have a lot of prey drive. But, with the proper training, this breed can be the most loyal and protective companion for a household."*

**Deborah Brown**
*Black Jade Rottweilers*

Though there is a lot more to this breed than just being a working dog, the Rottweiler's reputation as a hard worker is well earned. As a descendant of one of the breeds of dogs used by Roman legions, this canine has thousands of years of genetics that focus on protection and attack.

Photo Courtesy of
Urša Spruk

# A Long History As A Hardworking Dog

The origins of this particularly intriguing breed go back a few thousand years, with the earliest known Rottweiler ancestor considered by some to be the Molossus. This large, intelligent breed is likely related to the Italian Mastiff. Others think that the breed may have started with an Asian Mastiff breed. Whoever their ancestor really is, it is certain that Rottweilers' history began around this time from one of the Mastiff breeds that produced several large breeds that are still around today.

The Rottweilers' long history of working with people was established by agrarian people across the Roman Empire, and they were famously hardworking dogs that helped people survive during harsh winters and when crossing the Alps. They were also used as traveling companions because of their loyalty and protectiveness. Being associated with one of the most successful militaries in western history has given this breed a lineage that shows they can be quite aggressive when they believe it to be necessary. However, that is far from the only defining characteristic of the breed.

The breed's ancestors actually spent more time dealing with the legions' livestock than participating in battles. As the legions moved around taking over Europe, the large dogs traveled with them, ensuring that the troops had adequate food to continue their expansion across the continent. The dogs took care of the cattle so the soldiers could take care of other tasks. The Mo-

Photo Courtesy of Amanda Pittigher

**FUN FACT**
American Rottweiler
Club (ARC)

Founded in 1973,
the American Rottweiler Club (ARC)
is the American Kennel Club's (AKC)
officially recognized breed club for
Rottweilers in America. As the umbrel-
la club for all AKC-affiliated Rottweiler
clubs, the ARC maintains the Rottweiler
breed standard and upholds a high
standard for its members in all club-re-
lated activities.
Reference: https://www.am-
rottclub.org/

lossus was most frequently used as a means of protecting herds from wild animals and enemies.

The Mastiffs' endurance and protective nature were traits that the Romans wanted to keep, so they bred their best an-imals to create dogs that were perfect for given situations. As the Romans became more selec-tive in their breeding, different breeds were eventually created, including the Rottweiler.

After the fall of the Roman Empire, the dogs still worked alongside humans, doing large-ly the same tasks for the German tribes. They were very common around the town of Rottweil in modern-day Germany. Herders employed the dogs to manage the cattle, particularly when the owners left the countryside and headed to the town for markets. Rottweil became a hub for trade, which helped to keep the breed's visibility high and eventually led to the breed being named "Rottweiler." They were also called the Butcher's Dog of Rott-

weil because butchers used them to help take slaughtered cattle to differ-ent towns. With the smell of the meat attracting attention, it was absolute-ly necessary to have extra protection from wildlife. The dogs also served to deter thieves from targeting the trav-eling butchers because the butchers would tie their coins to the dogs' collars.

By the 19th century, the Rottwei-ler was incredibly popular, but with the beginning of the Industrial Revolution, many of the breed's uses became ob-solete. Trains made travel easy so that protection was no longer necessary. With the outlawing of cattle herding, there was no need for the breed to help manage the herds. The breed saw an in-

Photo Courtesy of
Shawn Maguire

Photo Courtesy of
Julie Buck

credibly sharp decline in their population, coming close to becoming extinct.

The turn of the century saw a new place for the few remaining Rottweilers. Crime began to rise in cities, and Rotties were both intimidating and intelligent, two personality traits that made them invaluable to police. In 1901, the standard Rottweiler look and temperament was established. Recognizing the risk of extinction, German breeders began to make sure that the breed was safeguarded. They recorded the desirable appearance and temperament of a Rottweiler, and these traits were documented to help other breeders meet the same standards and health for their pups.

By 1910, the breed became the fourth official police dog under the German Police Dog Association. The visibility of the Rottweiler helped it become popular as a working dog once more, branching out to work for the military and as guard dogs. They even helped the German military during World War I doing a wide range of dangerous tasks, such as being messengers and ambulance dogs (they would pull stretchers and help located wounded soldiers on the field).

The first Rottweiler club, the Allgemeiner Deutscher Rottweiler Klub, was established in 1921. Today, German Rottweilers tend to be bigger than most other versions of the breed, keeping more of the enormous size from their Mastiff origins. Around 1936 Thelma Gray took her Rottweiler to the UK. She continued to bring more Rottweilers to the UK until World War II began in 1939.

The next time Rottweilers were brought to the UK was in 1953. The popularity of the breed was not immediate, perhaps because of the dogs' intimidating appearance, plus the stigma of being a German breed – something that worked against them after the end of World War II. The UK Kennel Club finally registered the Rottweiler in 1965.

Rottweilers were recognized by the American Kennel Club (AKC) in 1931. This is because German emigrants brought the breed to the US during the 1920s and the first pups were born around 1930 in the US. By the next year, the breed was recognized and its popularity exploded because of their intelligence and loving nature. Rottweilers did have a dip in popularity during and immediately after World War II, but this didn't last long. By the middle of the 20th century, they were considered great pets because of their obedience and nurturing ways.

# A Common Breed On Restriction Lists And With Breed Legislation

While it is definitely true that Rottweilers, Dobermann Pinschers, and German Shepherds can be dangerous, this is true of any dog that is not properly trained. Their size and association with police and as a protective breed has resulted in them being considered dangerous. Easily one of the most obedient dogs in the world, the Rottweiler does not deserve the scary reputation that it currently has.

Unfortunately, Rottweilers are one of the breeds that is often subjected to legislation and restrictions. If you are considering adopting a Rottweiler (or any breed that is considered dangerous, whether its reputation is earned or not), you need to know what the laws are in your jurisdiction. If you are moving into a rental place, you will need to review the breed restrictions to make sure that Rottweilers are allowed. Despite this fact, the AKC has recorded the Rottweiler as America's eighth most popular breed. This shows that despite the breed's bad publicity, people realize that the dogs' poor reputation is not earned.

Photo Courtesy of
Tonya Renee Jones
Lakeview Kennel

## CHAPTER 2.

# Loyal, Loving Guardians – Determining If The Rottweiler Is The Right Breed For You

*"Rottweilers are extremely loyal. Their looks are intimidating but there's nothing more impressive than such a powerful breed that is truly a big teddy bear!"*

**Maria Bledsoe**
*JeMar Rottweilers*

Rottweilers are fantastic pets. It is incredibly difficult to find a better family dog if you love to be active and want a dog that will help you take care of your kids. They are protective, but not aggressive. They are loving and affectionate and great for most types of families.

*Photo Courtesy of
Johanna Steenkamp*

Photo Courtesy of
Brendan Burtnett

# Descriptions And Defining Characteristics

From their coloring to their unique appearance, Rottweilers look very intimidating. Then they open their mouths to show you a grin that is nearly impossible not to love.

## Appearance

Rottweilers are a large breed, typically ranging between 86 and 130 pounds with a height between 22 and 27 inches to their shoulders. The German Rottweilers are the biggest of the breed because of how early the standards were established in Germany, as well as the long history of the breed tied to the country. Regardless of their size, Rottweilers have a very sleek form with a lot of muscle, and both traits are highlighted by their glossy, short-haired coats.

What really distinguishes the Rottweiler is color. The breed's black coat has some brownish or rust-colored markings on the underside. The charming brown markings are most obvious on the face, but also run down the chest and legs. If the black coloring makes them look intimidating and helps the dogs blend into the dark, the rust color makes them look friendly, particularly as it highlights their eyebrows. When they open their mouths to pant, the extra colors around their eyes makes them look like they are smiling.

*Photo Courtesy of*
*Christine Hostetter*

Their sleek bodies are a result of their industrious history. When Rottweilers run, it is fairly hypnotic to watch them because of the way they effortlessly glide. They have a large chest and a more tapered frame than German Shepherd's body. In appearance, their bodies are most similar to that of a Boxer or Labrador Retriever.

The Rottweiler's head really isn't comparable to that of any other breed; rather, it is more like a mix of several other breeds, showing how it is closely related to many other large dogs that evolved from the Mastiffs that accompanied the Romans across Europe. Their ears are reminiscent of a Lab's, with the same kind of short fur around them. The face is much wider though, with a longish snout.

Until the 1990s, many people docked their Rottweiler's tail. Tail docking is removing part of the tail for purely cosmetic purposes, making it an unnecessary surgical practice. In 1997, the German Rottweiler organization banned docking as an acceptable practice. The only countries that did not follow the German ban are Canada and the US. There are strict regulations on docking though, with many states requiring that a specialist perform the operation.

## Temperament

It is rare to find a Rottweiler that scares easily, although unexpected noises can startle them. Despite their reputation, Rotties are not an aggressive breed as they tend to enjoy playing and going on adventures. Most of them are surprisingly calm, making them fantastic for families with young children as Rotties won't be too unnerved by the screaming and crying of the children.

With their families, Rottweilers tend to consider themselves as being lap dogs, and they want to be wherever you are. They don't require your full attention, but it will be rare when they don't follow you around the house to ensure they are in the same room as the rest of their pack.

Rottweilers are less open with strangers, particularly in their home, but they aren't prone to attacking people who come through the front door – unless it is with kisses and a desire for attention. Some Rottweilers can be territorial, which is why it is absolutely essential to socialize them at an early age. They tend to be a little more aloof than some of the large breeds, so you want to make sure they know that people and other dogs are acceptable guests.

If you want a guard dog for your family, there are few breeds that are as well-suited to the task as a Rottie. With their high level of endurance and confidence, this is a breed that has been trained for centuries to protect. When trained, they are more likely to observe before deciding if they need to act, which can take people by surprise. Rottweilers are not the kind to just jump to conclusions; they want to make sure they have the right course of action, then they act with confidence and tenacity.

Photo Courtesy of Darren Porter

Training is just as critical because Rotties are fairly active. Even if your pooch isn't aggressive, you don't want a large canine barreling through your home. Given how intelligent they are, training is usually fairly easy, giving you a way to help remove some of their energy. Chapters 10 and 13 go into more detail about training and exercises that are ideal for Rottweilers.

# Ideal Environment For Rottweilers

*"You should always remember that Rottweilers are a working breed and happiest when they have a job. They are versatile and excel in most dog venues. If you decide on a working breed then you should be ready to enjoy time with your pet and doing things with them, including on going to classes in obedience and other venues."*

**Kathryn Lovan**
*Halo Rottweilers*

Photo Courtesy of Courtney Bourg

Rottweilers can do well in nearly any kind of home, but they are large animals. If you let them on the couch, they will take up at least as much space as an adult. Therefore, a larger home tends to work best for the breed.

They have a lot of energy, so be prepared to make sure they have an outlet. Because Rotties can be territorial, you need to make certain that your dog understands that your home is not off limits to others. They have to learn to be less wary of people and animals coming into their home, which will mean more work during training. Chapter 8 covers what you need to do to properly socialize your Rottie, but for now know that you will need to have a space for your dog to stay when you have company or you will need to plan for training with every visitor.

## A Yard Isn't Necessary – But Your Dog Will Require Frequent Walks Without One

It isn't absolutely necessary to have a yard when you have a Rottweiler, but if you don't, you will need to plan for three to four long walks a day. You can do some inside training, but that won't be sufficient to tire out your puppy. Several daily walks are necessary, even if you do have a yard. Simply putting your dog outside and expecting your Rottie to get tired when he is alone is not going to happen.

Taking your dog somewhere new to play will help keep him both mentally and physically stimulated. This is advisable whether or not you have a yard. Hikes and jobs are also fantastic ways of making sure your Rottie gets adequate exercise.

> **FUN FACT**
> **Rottweiler Rescuers**
>
> In the days following the terror attacks on the World Trade Center on 9/11, over 300 search and rescue (SAR) dogs were employed to assist in the process of locating people trapped in the rubble. Among the hundreds of dogs who worked at Ground Zero, a handful were Rottweilers. The last known survivor found in the wreckage was found by a SAR dog 27 hours after the attack.

## Training And Socialization Are Required To Bring Out The Best In Your Rottweiler

Photo Courtesy of Faith Xiong

Though their reputation as a dangerous dog is not accurate in most cases, an unsocialized Rottweiler can be incredibly dangerous. The breed is naturally wary of strangers and doesn't like other pets entering its space. If not exposed to other people and animals from an early age, Rotties will likely be more aggressive when they get older because they do not naturally trust people and pets they do not know.

Without proper training, Rottweilers, due to their size, may run around knocking people and other pets over, which will make ev-

Photo Courtesy of
Stacy Schuckmann

eryone miserable. Just because your Rottweiler isn't likely to bite anyone doesn't mean he won't accidentally hurt someone if he pushes his way out of the house when the door opens.

## Do Your Research

*"The Rottweiler is a working breed and might possibly challenge his new owner. You need to be the alpha and establish the pecking order and must be capable of being the boss or leader at all times."*

**Maria Bledsoe**
*JeMar Rottweilers*

Rottweilers are not a good breed for first-time dog parents. They are amazing dogs, but it can take a lot of work to help them reach their full potential.

From activities to tire them out to the best training techniques if you are having problems, there is a lot that you will need to research before bringing your Rottie home. If you are uncertain that you will be able to handle such a confident and protective dog, save yourself and the dog the heartache of having to split up later. Like all intelligent, large dogs (even the gentle Retrievers), you have to have a firm hand and gain your Rottie's respect to ensure the dog is a happy addition to the home. Your Rottie is going to want to protect you, so you need to do your part to protect your Rottie from impulses that could be detrimental to your and your dog's happiness.

It is as important to determine if you are a good fit for your dog as it is to determine if your dog is a good fit for your home. The best owner for a Rottie is assertive and calm. Rotties also prefer a structured environment. A predictable schedule can keep them feeling at ease.

It is important to make time for your Rottie too, and not just for exercise. They love to be petted and played with. When they lean on you, that is their way of hugging you, and you should reciprocate. Though they may make great guard dogs and protectors, Rottweilers require attention and affection in exchange.

# CHAPTER 3.
# Finding Your Rottweiler

*"Temperament and health is paramount in making a good choice. See the puppy or dog in their environment and observe how they interact with adults, children and other animals."*

**Daviann Mitchell**
*Nighthawk Rottweilers*

If you are still reading this book, then you are probably certain that the Rottweiler is the dog for you – and with that decision comes a lot of excitement. Rotties have a lot to offer any family, especially if you want a dog that will act like a large teddy bear.

Finding the right Rottie can take quite a lot of time, but it is worth it. We do not recommend looking for your canine at a pet store or online, and you need to be careful of puppy mills. There are a number of red flags when it comes to finding the right dog, but there are several guaranteed ways to find a great new family member. Every breed comes with its own genetic issues, and this is part of why the hunt for your Rottie is going to take a while. You should find out about the puppy's parents to ensure that your puppy has the best chance of living a healthy, happy life. Given that their average lifespan is between 8 and 10 years, you want to work with a breeder who takes genetics seriously and works to minimize the risks that their puppies will have health problems.

*Photo Courtesy of
Hayley Lennox*

Photo Courtesy of
Lori Ann Manns

# Puppy Versus Adult

Deciding to adopt a Rottie is just the beginning. From there you need to decide whether you want to adopt a puppy or an adult. There are positive and negatives to both, just like with every breed. The approach to adopting a Rottweiler is the same as it is for most other breeds. However, with a protective dog like the Rottweiler, you are going to want to ask a lot more questions about adopting an adult than with other breeds.

## Adopting A Puppy

All puppies are a lot of work, starting with the moment the puppy enters your care. The personality and temperament of your Rottie is going to be based on how well you train and socialize your puppy. From the very beginning, you have to establish yourself and your family as the ones in charge so that your Rottie understands the hierarchy from the moment he enters your home. This can be exhausting because the dogs have a lot of energy from an early age.

The work to prepare for your puppy begins long before your puppy arrives. Puppy proofing the home is as time consuming as child proofing your home. While it is essential to puppy proof your home, you'll still have

*Photo Courtesy of Olivia Herold*

to keep a constant eye on your puppy after the little guy arrives. If you do not have the time to puppy proof your home, then you should consider getting an adult dog (you should probably also consider a different breed because a Rottweiler of any age brought into the home is going to be a large time investment).

Rottie pups are excitable and happy, but they aren't quite as robust as their adult counterparts. You have to be very careful and make sure that no one tries to pick up your puppy, which is quite difficult because of how similar they are to stuffed animals in appearance – Rottweiler puppies are absolutely adorable, not showing the powerful form that they will have later. Other than their intelligence, you can expect raising your puppy to be relatively similar to raising any other dog breed.

On the plus side, you will have more time to live together with a puppy than with an adult dog. You will have records about the puppy and the puppy's parents, making it easier to identify the potential problems your Rottie may suffer. This makes it considerably easier to ensure your puppy stays healthy and to catch potential issues earlier.

Some people find it easier to bond with puppies than with adult dogs. A young puppy is going to be nervous in a new home, but there isn't much risk of the puppy being dangerously aggressive. Your primary job will be protecting your puppy and making sure that you patiently train him. Training is absolutely essential with any protective breed because of how intelligent they are, so you will need to have a plan in place before your puppy arrives. We will cover this more in a later chapter.

## Rescuing A Rottie

*"When choosing a Rottweiler from a rescue, the most important factor is the temperament of that dog, because you won't know any of the dog's history. So having the dog temperament tested by a professional or someone familiar with the breed would be the best tip."*

**Teresa Bradley**
*Neu-Rodes Rottweilers*

Rescuing any dog comes with some inherent risks. While it is possible to find Rottie puppies at dog rescues, it is much more likely that you will find a rescued adult. Depending on the dog's age, you may need to consider the pros and cons of both adopting a puppy and rescuing an adult dog.

Adopting an older Rottweiler will require a lot of work to bring home, especially if you already have dogs and other animals. Rotties don't tend to be fond of other dogs, even if they have been socialized. Often there is an initial mistrust with other pets, but this can be overcome with patience and slowly helping them get accustomed to the other pets in the home.

As stated before, Rottweilers are intelligent, confident, calculating, and fearless. Adults who were not properly trained or socialized can be dangerous, though most rescue agencies will not have these higher risk Rottweilers up for adoption. Many Rottie-specific rescue organizations are cautious about adopting out a rescue with personality and socialization issues. Rescue shelters will be less careful, though they will

Photo Courtesy of Gillian Hall

definitely try to impress upon potential adopters the risks and problems they are likely to face with a specific Rottweiler.

The benefits of rescuing a Rottie are very similar to those of adopting any rescue dog. Many of them aren't bad dogs, they just have some bad habits. The odds are very good that you aren't going to be starting from scratch with housetraining – which can be a huge plus for most people who don't have time to train a stubborn puppy. Adult dogs are awake more often than puppies, and while it may take them a bit longer to warm up to you, you can bond much faster with an adult, depending on their age. Adult Rotties will be more wary of you, so you need to create an environment that feels safe and comfortable to your new family member. Your new dog is not likely to want to cuddle with you in the early days either, which may be a bit dispiriting. Don't worry. Once your adult dog bonds with you, it will be like flipping an affection switch, and then you really could not ask for a more loving canine.

One thing that is similar to preparing your home for puppies is that you will want to dog proof your home for a rescue. You will need to have everything set up before the dog arrives – most people think it isn't necessary to prepare for an adult dog and fail to properly prepare. It will just be less time consuming than preparing a home for a puppy. You should not keep the Rottie adult locked up in a crate the majority of the time, so at least in the beginning you will need a large space for the dog to get familiar with you and your home as you assess the personality and capabilities. It is a fairly important consideration, particularly if you have other dogs, as you want to ensure harmony in the home.

You may not be able to get a complete health record for an adult Rottweiler, but it is more likely that you will find a dog that has already been spayed or neutered, as well as chipped. Unless you adopt a Rottie that has health issues (these should be disclosed by the rescue organization, but probably won't be available for some rescues), rescues tend to be less costly at the first office visit to the vet than puppies.

Older dogs give you more immediate gratification. You don't have to go through those sleepless nights with a new puppy or the endless frustration that comes with early types of training. Older Rottweilers let you get right into enjoying your dog as you go out on adventures, even if there is a period of mistrust and uncertainty. All intelligent, high energy dogs require a lot of time and attention as puppies. Bypassing that is a major part of the appeal of older dogs.

## Rottweiler Clubs And Rescues

There is a wealth of Rottweiler clubs and rescues. If you know German, you should definitely check out the original Rottweiler club to get as much information and details about the breed. To start your search, here are the best places to begin in North America:

- American Rottweiler Club (an American Kennel Club affiliate)
- Colonial Rottweiler Club
- Rottweiler Club of Canada
- Gulfstream Rottweiler Club of Greater Miami
- Dogwood Rottweiler Club of Metropolitan Atlanta Georgia
- Greater Rochester Rottweiler Club
- Medallion Rottweiler Club
- Emerald Valley Rottweiler Club of Greater Cleveland
- Mile High Rottweiler Club
- Golden State Rottweiler Club
- Associated Rottweiler Fanciers of Northern California
- Southwestern Rottweiler Club of San Diego
- Western Rottweiler Owners
- The Rottweiler Club of Alaska
- Southern States Rottweiler Rescue
- NoVa Rottweiler Rescue League, Inc.
- North East Rottweiler Rescue
- Big Sky Rottweiler Rescue
- Gulfstream Guardian Angels Rottweiler Rescue, Inc.
- MidAmerica Rottweiler Rescue
- Rottweiler Hearts Rescue
- Rising Star Rottweiler Rescue, Inc.
- Rotten Rottie Rescue

# Adopting From A Breeder

As an established breed with a well-documented history for the last century, Rottweilers' genetic issues are well known. This means that responsible breeders should be working to reduce potential issues and this includes tracking the genetic history of their dogs in order to prevent inherited ailments from being passed along to puppies.

## Health Tests And Certifications

Larger breeds tend to have more health problems because of their size, which is why they tend to have shorter life expectancies than smaller dogs. Unfortunately, Rottweilers are no exception. When looking for a Rottie to adopt, there are a number of health concerns that you should ask breeders or rescue groups about.

The following are health tests all breeders should ensure their Rotties undergo:

- Cardiac exam (OFA evaluation)
- Hip Evaluation
- Elbow Evaluation
- Eye examination by someone who is a member of the ACVO Ophthalmologist (they should be registered with either the OFA or the CERF)

Breeders who take the time to join one of the many Rottweiler clubs or organizations prove that they are serious about the health of their puppies. Many of these organizations require that a standardized set of requirements be met, so membership denotes the breeders who join the organizations as reliable and reputable.

## Contracts And Guarantees

Though Rottweilers' potential genetic problems are very well known, it is impossible to completely eliminate all of the risks. Breeder contracts and guarantees are meant to protect the puppies as much as they are meant to protect you.

If a breeder has a contract that must be signed, make sure that you read through it completely and are willing to meet all of the requirements prior to signing it. The contracts tend to be fairly easy to understand and comply with, but you should be aware of all the facts before you agree to anything. Beyond putting down the money for the puppy, signing the contract says that you are serious about how you plan to take care of the puppy to the best of your abilities by meeting the minimum requirements set forth by the breeder. A contract may also say that the breeder will retain the puppy's original registration papers, although you can get a copy of the papers.

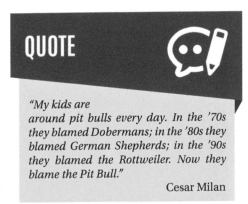

*"My kids are around pit bulls every day. In the '70s they blamed Dobermans; in the '80s they blamed German Shepherds; in the '90s they blamed the Rottweiler. Now they blame the Pit Bull."*

Cesar Milan

The guarantee states what health conditions the breeder promises for their puppies. This typically includes details of the dog's health and recommendations on the next steps of the puppy's care once it leaves the breeder's facility. Guarantees may also provide schedules to ensure that the health care started by the breeder is continued by the new puppy parent. In the event that a major health concern is found, the puppy will need to be returned to the breeder. The contract will also explain what is not guaranteed. The guarantee tends to be very long (sometimes longer than the contract), and you should read it thoroughly before you sign.

Rottie contracts usually come with a requirement to have the dog spayed or neutered once it reaches maturity (typically six months). The contract may also contain naming requirements, health details, and a stipulation for what will happen if you can no longer take care of the animal (the dog usually goes back to the breeder). They also include information on what will happen if you are negligent or abusive to your dog.

## Puppy Genetics – The Parents

*"You need to know the background of the linage on the pup to get an indication of what they will be like as they grow. I suggest that you find out about the parents of your Rottweiler, because the puppy will get 70% of it traits from its parents."*

**Bobby and Melissa Kemp**
*Gold Hill Kennels*

A healthy puppy requires healthy parents and a clean genetic history. A good breeder keeps extensive records of each puppy and their parents. You will want to review each of the parents' complete history to understand what traits your puppy is likely to inherit. Pay attention to learning abilities, temperament, clinginess, and any personality trait you consider important. You can either request documents be sent electronically to you or get them when you visit the breeder in person.

It could take a while to review the breeder's information about each parent, but it is always well worth the time you spend studying and planning. The more you know about the parents, the better prepared you will be for your puppy. The great breeders will have stories and details about the parents so that you can read about them at your leisure.

## Finding A Breeder

Now that you know some of the basics of what to expect, it is time to start talking to breeders. The goal is to determine which breeders are willing to take the time to patiently and thoroughly answer all of your questions. They should have as much love for their Rottweilers as they want you to feel for your new puppy. And they should want to make sure that their puppies go to good homes.

If you find someone who posts regular pictures and information about the parents and the progress of the mother's pregnancy and vet visits, that is a very good sign. The best breeders will not only talk about their dogs and the plans for the parents in the future, they will stay in contact with you after you take the puppy home and answer any questions as they arise. These are the kinds of breeders who are likely to have waiting lists. The active interest in knowing about what happens to the puppies later shows that they care a great deal about each individual dog.

It is likely that for each breeder you call, the conversation will last about an hour. If a breeder does not have time to talk and isn't willing to talk with you later, you can cross them off your list. After you have talked with each of your possible breeders, compare their answers. With a breed like the Rottweiler, there are some variations in personalities based on what the parents are like. If you want a dog that is more easily trained, you want parents that are more intelligent and less stubborn to increase the likelihood that your puppy will be easier to train.

The following are some questions to ask. Make sure that you have pen and paper or your computer handy.

- Ask if you can visit in person. The answer should always be yes, and if it isn't, you don't need to ask any further. Thank them and hang up. Even if the breeder is located in a different state, they should allow you to visit the facility.

- Ask about the required health tests and certifications they have for their puppies. These points are detailed further in the next section, so make sure to check off the available tests and certifications for each breeder. If they don't have all of the tests and certifications, you may want to remove them from consideration.

- Make sure that the breeder always takes care of all of the initial health requirements in the first few weeks through the early months, particularly shots. Puppies require certain procedures before they leave their mother to ensure they are healthy. Vaccinations and worming typically start around six weeks after the puppies are born, then need to be continued every three weeks. By the time your puppy is old enough to come home, he should be well into the procedures, or even completely through with the first phases of these important health care needs.

- Ask if the puppy is required to be spayed or neutered before reaching a certain age of maturity. Typically, these procedures are done in the puppies' best interest.

- Find out if the breeder is part of a Rottweiler organization or group.

- Ask about the first phases of your puppy's life, such as how the breeder plans to care for the puppy during those first few months. They should be able to provide a lot of detail, and they should do this without sounding as though they are irritated that you want to know. They will also let you know how much training you can expect to be done prior to the puppy's arrival in your home so you can plan to take over as soon as the puppy arrives. It is possible that the breeder may start housetraining the puppy. You will want to find out if they can provide information on how quickly the puppies have picked up on the training. You want to be able to pick up from where the breeder left off once your Rottweiler reaches your home.

- See what kind of advice the breeder gives about raising your Rottweiler puppy. They should be more than happy to help guide you to doing what is best for your dog because they will want the puppies to live happy, healthy lives. You should also be able to rely on a breeder's recommendations, advice, and additional care after the puppy arrives at your home. Basically, you are getting customer support, as well as a great chance of a healthy dog. Breeders who show a lot of interest in the dog's well-being and are willing to answer questions during the dog's entire life span are likely to breed puppies that are healthy.

- How many breeds do they manage a year? How many sets of parents do the breeders have? Puppies can take a lot of time and attention, and the mother should have some down time between pregnancies. Learn about the breeder's standard operations to find out if they are taking care of the parents and treating them like valuable family members and not as strictly a way to make money.

## Selecting Your Puppy

*"Choose a dog who is 1) Structurally sound, 2) Has a solid temperament, and 3) Has the amount of drive you are looking for."*

**Elissa O'Sullivan**
*Falkore Rottweilers*

Selecting your puppy should be done in person. However, you can start checking out your puppy after birth if the breeder is willing to share videos and pictures. When you are finally allowed to see the puppies in person, there are several things you need to check the puppies for before making your final decision. Some of the things that you are looking are universal, regardless of breed, and other things are Rottweiler specific.

- Assess the group of puppies as a whole. If most or all of the puppies are aggressive or fearful, this is an indication of a problem with the litter or (more likely) the breeder. Here are a few red flags if displayed by a majority of the puppies

Photo Courtesy of Danielle Ingram

  - Tucked tails

  - Shrinking away from people

  - Whimpering when people get close

  - Constant attacking of your hands or feet (beyond pouncing)

- If you have dogs at home, notice how well each puppy plays with the others. This is a great indicator of just how well your puppy will react to any pets you already have.

- Notice which puppies greet you first, and which hang back to observe.

- The puppies should not be fat or underweight, which admittedly, can be difficult to tell with their coats. A swollen stomach is generally a sign of worms or other health problems.

- Puppies should have straight, sturdy legs. Splayed legs can be a sign that there is something wrong.
- Examine the puppy's ears for mites, which will cause discharge. The inside of the ear should be pink, not red or inflamed.
- The eyes should be clear and bright.
- Check the puppy's mouth for pink, healthy looking gums.
- Pet the puppy to check his coat for the following.
  - Ensure that the coat feels thick and full. If the breeders have allowed the fur to get matted or really dirty, it is an indication that they likely are not taking proper care of the animals.
  - Check for fleas and mites by running your hand from the head to the tail, then under the tail (fleas are more likely to hide under most dogs' tails). Mites may look like dandruff.
- Check the puppy's rump for redness and sores, and see if you can check the last bowel movement to ensure it is firm.

Pick the puppy that exhibits the personality traits that you want in your dog. If you want a forward, friendly, excitable dog, the first puppy to greet you may be the one you seek. If you want a dog that will think things through and let others get more attention, look for a puppy who sits back and observes you before approaching.

# CHAPTER 4.
# **Preparing For Your Puppy**

It takes months to prepare a home for a puppy, and there is still plenty to do during those last few weeks. Be prepared for it to take about as long as if you were bringing a baby into the home, with many of the same concerns. Making sure your new Rottweiler has a safe space with all of the essentials (especially toys) will make the arrival of your newest family addition a great time for everyone – especially your new canine companion.

*Photo Courtesy of*
*Sonia Howard*

# Preparing Your Kids

*"Rottweilers love children!  Kids become 'theirs' and they will be very protective of them."*

**Grace Acosta**
*Acosta Rottweilers*

You want your pup to feel comfortable from the beginning, which means making sure any children are careful and gentle. Begin to prepare your kids as soon as you plan to adopt your Rottweiler – even if you plan to get an adult.

You will need to be ready to refresh these rules regularly, both before the puppy arrives and after the arrival. The first time your kids begin to play with the puppy, you will need to be present, and you cannot leave them alone. You will actually need to stay with your children when they interact with the puppy for several months, or longer, depending on the kids' age. Older teens will probably be all right to help with the puppy, but younger teens and kids should not be left alone with the puppy for a few months. Remember that you will need to be very firm to make sure that the puppy is not hurt or frightened.

The following are the five golden rules that you want to make sure your children follow from the very first interaction.

1. Always be gentle.

2. Chase is an outside game.

3. Always leave the puppy alone during mealtime.

4. The Rottweiler should always remain firmly on the ground.

5. All of your valuables should be kept well out of the puppy's reach.

Since your kids are going to ask why, here are the explanations you can give them. You can simplify them for younger kids, or start a dialogue with teens.

**HELPFUL TIP**
**Breed Restrictions**

In some places, Rottweilers have gained a reputation for being dangerous and aggressive, most likely because these dogs have sometimes been bred as fighting dogs. While proper training and care make Rottweilers excellent pets, the stigma can mean that certain cities or landlords have bans on the breed. Be sure to check with your local ordinances or landlord before bringing your puppy home.

*Photo Courtesy of Shayna Lammers*

## Always Be Gentle

Little Rottweiler puppies are absolutely adorable, but they are also fairly fragile, despite their rugged appearance. At no time should anyone play rough with the puppy (or any adult Rottweiler).

This rule must be applied consistently every time your children play with the puppy. Be firm if you see your children getting too excited or rough. You don't want the puppy to get overly excited either because he might end up nipping or biting. If he does, it isn't his fault because he hasn't learned better yet – it is a child's fault. Make sure your children understands the possible repercussions if they get too rough.

## Chase

It can be easy for children to forget as they start to play and everyone gets excited. That short game of getting away can quickly devolve into chase, so you will need to make sure your children understand not to start running. Once they get outside, chasing is perfectly fine (though you will still need to monitor the play time).

Running inside the home is dangerous for two primary reasons. It gives your Rottweiler puppy the impression that your home isn't safe inside because he is being chased. Or your puppy will learn that running inside is fine, which can be very dangerous as the gets older. One of the last things you want is for your Rottweiler to go barreling through your home knocking people off their feet because it was fine for him to do that when he was a puppy.

## Mealtime

Rottweilers aren't typically aggressive, so it isn't likely they will nip or bite because someone is near their food. However, they can feel insecure about eating if they feel like someone may take their food away, which is obviously not fair to your Rottweiler. And older Rottweilers can be a bit more protective of their food, which could lead to some conflicts. Save yourself, your family, and your Rottweiler trouble by making sure everyone knows that eating time is your Rottweiler's time alone. Similarly, teach your kids that their own mealtime is off limits to the puppy. No feeding him from the table.

## Paws On The Ground

This is something that will likely require a good bit of explaining to your children as Rottweilers look a lot like toys, especially Rottweiler puppies. No one should be picking the puppy up off the ground. You may want to carry your new family member around or play with the pup like a baby, but you and your family will need to resist that urge. Kids particularly have trouble understanding since they will see the Rottweiler puppy more like a toy than a living creature. The younger your children are, the more difficult it will be for them to un-

Photo Courtesy of
Courtney Bourg

*Photo Courtesy of Howard Jones*

derstand the difference. It is so tempting to treat the Rottweiler like a baby and to try to carry it like one, but this is incredibly uncomfortable and unhealthy for the puppy. Older kids will quickly learn that a puppy nip or bite hurts a lot more than you would think. Those little teeth are incredibly sharp, and you don't want the puppy to be dropped. If your children learn never to pick up the puppy, things will go a lot better. Remember, this also applies to you, so don't make things difficult by doing something you constantly tell your children not to do.

## Keep Valuables Out Of Reach

Valuables are not something you want to end up in the puppy's mouth, whether that's toys, jewelry, shoes, etc. Your kids will be less than happy if their personal possessions are chewed up by an inquisitive puppy, so teach them to put toys, clothes, and other valuables far out of the puppy's reach.

# Preparing Your Current Dogs

Rottweilers tend to be wary of other dogs. When they are puppies, you have a chance to start socializing them with your other dogs, but you will need to be careful to make sure that they have a great experience.

This means if you already have canines in your home, they are going to need to be prepared for the new arrival.

Here are the important tasks to prepare your current pets for your new arrival.

- Set a schedule for the things you will need to do and the people who will need to participate.
- Preserve your current dogs' favorite places and furniture, and make sure their toys and items are not in the puppy's space.
- Have play dates at your home and analyze your dogs to see how they react.

## Set A Schedule

Establish a schedule that you will keep once the puppy arrives. This lets your current furry companions know that they are still loved after a puppy arrives. Obviously, the puppy is going to get a lot of attention, so you need to make a concerted effort to let your current canine know that you still love and care for him. Basically, you are making time in your schedule just for your current dog or dogs, and you will need to make sure that you don't stray from that schedule after the puppy's arrival.

Make sure that you plan to have at least one adult around for each other dog you have. Cats are generally less of a concern, but you will probably want to have at least one adult around when the puppy comes home. We will go into more detail later about what the roles of the other adults will be, but for now, when you know what date you will be bringing your puppy home, make sure that you have adults who know to be present to help. You may need to remind them as the time nears, so set an alert on your phone for that, as well as the date, time, and pickup information for your puppy.

One benefit of having a schedule for your other dogs in place before your Rottie puppy arrives is that it will be easy to keep a schedule with the puppy. Rottweilers love to know what to expect. Your other dogs can help you adapt to that so that you can better support your puppy from the beginning.

Your puppy is going to eat, sleep, and spend most of the day and night in his assigned space. This means that the space cannot block your current canine from her favorite furniture, bed, or any place where she rests over the course of the day. None of your current dog's stuff should be in this area, and this includes toys. You don't want your dog to feel like the puppy is taking over her territory. Make sure your children understand to never to put your current dog's stuff in the puppy's area as well.

Your dog and the puppy will need to be kept apart in the early days, (even if they seem friendly) until your puppy is done with vaccinations. Puppies are more susceptible to illness during these days, so wait until the puppy is protected before the dogs spend time together.

*Photo Courtesy of Megan Bartz Offord*

## Getting An Idea How Your Dogs Will React – Extra At Home Playdates

Here are things that will best help prepare your pooch for the arrival of your puppy.

- Think about your dog's personality to help you decide the best way to prepare for that first day, week, and month. Each dog is unique, so you will need to consider your dog's personality to determine how things will go when the new dog arrives. If your current dog loves other dogs, this will probably hold true when the puppy shows up. If your dog has any territorial tendencies, you will need to be cautious about the introduction and first couple of months so that your current dog learns that the Rottweiler is now a part of the pack. Excitable dogs will need special attention to keep them from getting overly agitated when a new dog comes home. You don't want them to be so excited they accidentally hurt the new Rottweiler.

- Consider the times when you have had other dogs in your home and how your current dog reacted to these other furry visitors. If your canine displayed territorial tendencies, you will need to be extra careful with how you introduce your new pup. If you haven't invited another dog to your home, have a couple of play dates with other dogs at your home before your new Rottweiler arrives. You have to know how your current fur babies will react to new dogs in the house so you can properly prepare. Meeting a dog at home is very different from encountering one outside the home.

- Think about your dog's interactions with other dogs for as long as you have known the pup. Has your dog shown either protective or possessive behavior, either with you or others? Food is one of the reasons most dogs will display some kind of aggression because they don't want anyone trying to eat what is theirs. Some dogs can be protective of people and toys too.

The same rules apply, no matter how many dogs you have. Think about the personalities of all of them as individuals, as well as how they interact together. Just like people, you may find that when they are together your dogs act differently, which you will need to keep in mind as you plan their first introduction.

See chapter 9 for planning to introduce your current dogs and your new puppy, and how to juggle a new puppy and your current pets.

*Photo Courtesy of Terri Kenney*

# Preparing A Puppy Space

Your puppy is going to need a dedicated space that includes a crate (you will need a small one in the beginning, but later you are going to need to upgrade to something bigger), food and water bowls, pee pad, and toys. This will need to be in an area where the puppy will be when you are not able to give dedicated attention. The puppy space should be safe and gated so that the puppy cannot get out, and young children and dogs cannot get in. It should be a safe space where the puppy can see you going about your usual business, and feel comfortable during the first night.

# Dangerous Foods

Dogs can eat raw meat without having to worry about the kinds of problems a person will encounter. However, there are human foods that could be fatal to your Rottweiler. You should keep these foods away from all dogs:

- Apple seeds
- Chocolate
- Coffee

- Cooked bones (they can kill a dog when the bones splinter in the dog's mouth or stomach)
- Corn on the cob (it is the cob itself that is deadly to dogs; corn off the cob is fine)
- Grapes/raisins
- Macadamia nuts
- Onions and chives
- Peaches, persimmons, and plums
- Tobacco (your Rottweiler will not know that it is not a food and may eat it if it's left out)
- Xylitol (a sugar substitute in candies and baked goods)
- Yeast

In addition to these potentially deadly foods, there is a long list of things that your dog shouldn't eat for health reasons. The Canine Journal has a lengthy list of foods that should be avoided.

# Hazards To Fix

Preparing for a puppy is time consuming, and all of the most dangerous rooms and items in your home will be equally as dangerous to your puppy as they are to a baby. The biggest difference is that your Rottweiler is going to be mobile much faster than a child, potentially getting into dangerous situations within a few weeks if you don't eliminate all of the dangers ahead of your puppy's arrival.

In the months leading up to your puppy's arrival, you'll need to make your home safe for his arrival. Be aware that Rottweilers (puppies in general) will try to eat virtually anything, even if it isn't food. Nothing is safe – not even your furniture. Puppies will gnaw on wood and metal. Anything within their reach is fair game. Keep this in mind as you go about puppy-proofing your home.

## Indoor Fixes

This section details the areas inside your home where you should focus your attention. In case of problems, have your vet's number posted to the fridge and at least one other room in the house. If you set this up before your pup arrives, it will be there if you need it. Even if you program it into your phone, another family member or someone taking care of your Rottie may need the number.

| Hazards | Fixes | Time Estimate |
|---|---|---|
| **Kitchen** | | |
| Poisons | Keep in secured, childproof cabinets or on high shelves | 30 min |
| Trash cans | Have a lockable trashcan, or keep it in a secured location | 10 min |
| Appliances | Make sure all cords are out of reach | 15 min |
| Human Food | Keep out of reach | Constant (start making it a habit) |
| **Floors** | | |
| Slippery surfaces | Put down rugs or special mats designed to stick to the floor | 30 min – 1 hour |
| Training area | Train on non-slippery surfaces | Constant |
| **Bathrooms** | | |
| Toilet brush | Either have one that locks or keep out of reach | 5 min/bathroom |
| Poisons | Keep in secured, childproof cabinets or on high shelves | 15 - 30 min/ bathroom |
| Toilets | Keep closed | |
| Do not use automatic toilet cleaning chemicals | Constant (start making it a habit) | |
| Cabinets | Keep locked with childproof locks | 15 - 30 min/ bathroom |
| **Laundry Room** | | |
| Clothing | Store clean and dirty clothing off the floor, out of reach | 15 – 30 min |
| Poisons (bleach, pods/detergent, dryer sheets, and misc. poisons) | Keep in secured, childproofed cabinets or on high shelves | 15 min |
| **Around the Home** | | |
| Plants | Keep off the floor | 45 min – 1 hour |
| Trash cans | Have a lockable trashcan, or keep it in a secured location | 30 min |
| Electrical cords, window blind cords | Hide them or makes sure they are out of reach; pay particular attention to entertainment and computer areas | 1.5 hours |

| Poisons | Check to make sure there aren't any (WD40, window/screen cleaner, carpet cleaner, air fresheners); move all poisons to a centralized, locked location | 1 hour |
|---|---|---|
| Windows | Check that cords are out of reach in all rooms | 1 – 2 hours |
| Fireplaces | Store cleaning supplies and tools where the puppy can't get into them; Cover the fireplace opening with something the puppy can't knock over | 10 min/fireplace |
| Stairs | Cordoned off so that your puppy cannot try to go up or down them; make sure to test gates/blocks | 10 – 15 min |
| Coffee tables/End tables/Nightstands | Clear of dangerous objects (e.g., scissors, sewing equipment, pens, and pencils) and all valuables | 30 – 45 min |

If you have a cat, keep the litter box off the floor. It needs to be somewhere that your cat can easily get to but your Rottweiler cannot. Since this involves teaching your cat to use the new area, it's something you should do well in advance of the puppy's arrival. You don't want your cat to undergo too many significant changes all at once. The puppy will be enough of a disruption – if your cat associates the litter box change with the puppy, you may find your cat protesting the change by refusing to use the litter box.

Rottweilers can get into nearly everything at their height, and they will be exploring a lot when given the opportunity. Anything that may catch your attention or draw your interest is worth a try – that's what centuries have taught them. Being vigilant about making sure they can't hurt themselves is vital to keeping your Rottweiler safe.

Your Rottie is going to figure out how to do things you don't want him to do. This could range from getting into an open toilet (which is why you cannot have automatic-chemical rinses) to crawling into cabinets or pantries. As intelligent as the breed is, it's best to overestimate what your puppy can do and prepare accordingly.

Get low and see each room from your Rottie's perspective. You are almost guaranteed to find at least one thing you missed.

# Outdoor Fixes

This section details the things outside your home that need your attention ahead of your puppy's arrival. Also post the vet's number in one of the sheltered areas in case of an emergency.

| Hazards | Fixes | Time Estimate |
|---|---|---|
| **Garage** | | |
| Poisons | Keep in secured, childproofed cabinets or on high shelves (e.g., car chemicals, cleaning, paint, lawn care) – this includes fertilizer | 1 hour |
| Trash bins | Keep it in a secured location | 5 min |
| Tools (e.g., lawn, car, hardware, power tools) | Make sure all cords are out of reach: Keep out of reach and never hanging over the side of surfaces | 30 min – 1 hour |
| Equipment (e.g., sports, fishing) | Keep out of reach and never hanging over the side of surfaces | Constant (start making it a habit) |
| Sharp implements | Keep out of reach and never hanging over the side of surfaces | 30 min |
| Bikes | Store off the ground or in a place the Rottie cannot get to (to keep the pup from biting the tires) | 20 min |
| **Fencing (Can Be Done Concurrently)** | | |
| Breaks | Fix any breaks in the fencing | 30 min - 1 hour |
| Gaps | Fill any gaps, even if they are intentional, so your Rottie doesn't escape | 30 min - 1 hour |
| Holes/Dips at Base | Fill any area that can be easily crawled under | 1 – 2 hours |
| **Yard** | | |
| Poisons | Don't leave any poisons in the yard | 1 – 2 hours |
| Plants | Verify that all low plants aren't poisonous to dogs; fence off anything that is (such as grape vines) | 45 min – 1 hour |
| Tools (e.g., lawn maintenance and gardening tools) | Make sure they are out of reach; Make sure nothing is hanging over outdoor tables | 30 min – 1 hour |

Never leave your Rottweiler alone in the garage, even as an adult. It is likely that your puppy will be in the garage when you take car trips, which is why it is important to puppy proof it. You should always have an eye on the dog, but you obviously can't climb under the car and will have a hard time getting into smaller spaces if your Rottie makes a break for it to explore – adult Rottweilers may be too big, but as puppies they are small enough to get into all kinds of tiny spaces.

Just like inside, you will need to follow up your outdoor preparations by getting low and checking out all areas from a puppy's perspective. Again, you are all but guaranteed to find at least one thing you missed.

# Supplies And Tools To Purchase And Prepare

*"Buy food and water bowls that are flared on bottom to prohibit them from turning over while your Rottweiler is eating.  That can avoid some big messes."*

**Charles Robinson**
*Von Euro Kennel*

Planning for your puppy's arrival means buying a lot supplies up front. You will need a wide range of items. If you start making purchases around the time you identify the breeder, you can stretch out your expenses over a longer period of time. This will make it seem a lot less expensive than it actually is, though it is much cheaper than what is needed for most other breeds. The following are recommended items:

- Crate
- Bed
- Leash
- Doggie bags for walks
- Collar
- Tags
- Puppy food
- Water and food bowls (sharing a water bowl is usually okay, but your puppy needs his or her own food dish if you have multiple dogs)
- Toothbrush/Toothpaste
- Brush
- Toys
- Training treats

Health care items like flea treatments can be purchased, but they are expensive and you won't need them for a while. Puppies should not be treated until they reach a specified age. Talk to your vet before buying any medications.

# Choosing Your Vet

You can start looking around for a vet for your Rottweiler even before you choose a breeder. This is a task that you can do when you have time, but it must be done at least a few weeks before your Rottie arrives. Whether you get a puppy or an adult, you should take your canine to the vet within 48 hours (24 hours is strongly recommended) of his arrival. Getting an appointment with a vet can take a while, just like getting a doctor's appointment, so you will need to have your vet and the first appointment booked well in advance.

Here are some things to consider when looking for a vet.

- What is their level of familiarity with Rottweilers? They don't have to be specialists, but you do want them to have some experience with the breed.
- How far from your home is the vet? You don't want the vet to be more than 30 minutes away in case of emergency.
- Is the vet available for emergencies after hours or can they recommend a vet in case of an emergency?
- Is the vet part of a local vet hospital if needed, or does the doctor refer patients to a local pet hospital?
- Is the vet the only vet or one of several partners? If he or she is part of a partnership, can you stick with just one vet for visits?
- How are appointments booked?
- Can you have other services performed there, such as grooming and boarding?
- Is the vet accredited?
- What are the prices for the initial visit and the normal costs, such as shots and regular visits?
- What tests and checks are performed during the initial visit?

Make time to visit the vet you are considering using so that you can look around to see what the environment is inside the office. See if you can speak to the vet to see if he or she is willing to help put you at ease and answer your questions. A vet's time is valuable, but they should have a few minutes to help you feel confident that they are the right choice to help take care of your canine.

# Planning The First Year's Budget

The budget for a puppy is a lot more than you would think – but it's still less expensive to bring a puppy home than a new infant. You will need to have a budget, which is another reason to start purchasing supplies a few months in advance. When you buy the items you need, you will begin to see exactly how much you will spend a month. Of course there are some items that are one-time purchases, such as a crate, but many other items will need to be purchased regularly, like food and treats.

Begin budgeting the day you decide to get your puppy. The cost will include the adoption cost, which is typically higher for a purebred dog than for a rescue.

The vet and other healthcare costs should be included in your budget. Regular vaccinations are required, and an annual checkup should be included in the budget.

If you want to join a Rottweiler organization, budget for that. There are a lot of things you can do with Rottweilers if you want to be with other puppy parents. Taking the time to training with other dogs is actually advised for the Rottie because they need as much positive socialization as possible in the early days. Taking classes with other dogs helps familiarize your puppy with other dogs in a safe environment. More details will be provided in a later chapter; for now it is important to budget this extra expense so that you can get your pup the socialization needed to help make your puppy comfortable around other dogs.

The following table can help you start to plan your budget. Keep in mind that the prices are a rough average, and may be significantly different based on where you live.

| Item | Considerations | Estimated Costs |
|------|----------------|-----------------|
| Crate | You will need two crates: one for the puppy and one for when the puppy grows up. This should be a comfortable space where the puppy will sleep and rest. | Wire crates: Range $60 to $350<br><br>Portable crate: Range $35 to $200 |
| Bed | You will probably need two beds: one for the puppy, and one for when the pup grows up. This will be placed in the crate. | $10 to $55 |

| Leash | It should be short in the beginning because you need to be able to keep your puppy from getting overexcited and running to the end of a long line. | Short leash: $6 to $15<br><br>Retractable: $8 to $25 |
|---|---|---|
| Doggie bags for walks | If you walk at parks, this won't be necessary. For those who don't have daily access to bags, it is best to purchase packs to ensure you don't run out of bags. | Singles cost less than $1 each.<br><br>Packs: $4 to $16 |
| Collar | You will likely need two collars: one for the puppy, and one for an adult Rottweiler. | $10 to $30 |
| Tags | These will likely be provided by your vet. Find out what information the vet provides for tags, then purchase any tags that are not provided. At a minimum, your Rottie should have tags with your address on it in case the pup escapes. | Contact your vet before purchasing to see if the required rabies tags include your contact info. |
| Puppy food | This one is going to depend on if you make your Rottie food, if you purchase food, or both. The larger the bag, the higher the cost, but the fewer times you will need to purchase food. You will need to purchase puppy specific food in the beginning, but will stop after the second year. Adult dog food is more expensive, particularly for large breeds like the Rottweiler | $9 to $90 per bag |
| Water and food bowls | These will need to be kept in the puppy's area. If you have other dogs, you will need separate bowls for the puppy. | $10 to $40 |
| Toothbrush/ Toothpaste | You will need to brush regularly, so plan to use more than one toothbrush during the first year. | $2.50 t0 $14 |

| Brush | Rottie coats are incredibly easy to maintain, but you should still brush them regularly. When they are puppies, brushing offers a great way to bond. | $3.50 to $20 |
|---|---|---|
| Toys | You definitely want to get your puppy toys, and you are going to want toys for more aggressive chewers, even if your puppy goes them remarkably quickly. You will want to keep getting your Rottie toys as an adult for play (cost of adult dog toys not included). | $2.00<br><br>Packs of toys range from $10 to $20 (easier in the long run as your pup will chew through toys quickly) |
| Training treats | You will need those from the beginning, and likely won't need to change the treats based on your Rottie's age; you may need to change treats to keep your dog's interest though. | $4.50to $15 |

You won't need to purchase the adult version of these items before the puppy arrives, but you will need to have them within the first 6 months because your puppy is going to grow fast. Set up a budget for the initial costs, then a second budget for adult versions of items that will need to be replaced as the puppy grows.

# CHAPTER 5
# **Bringing Home Your Rottweiler**

*"Rottweiler puppies are full of energy and full of mischief. They can also be very determined. Remember with proper training and patience you will be rewarded with the very best friend you will ever have."*

**Kathryn Lovan**
*Halo Rottweilers*

Your new Rottweiler will be ready for training pretty much from the time he enters your care. Obviously a puppy is going to have a much more limited attention span, but Rottie puppies are both smart and eager enough to want to learn – even if they are a bit apprehensive in the early days when they leave their mother.

Bringing home a puppy is a bit like bringing home a newborn – one that can already learn, but is still very much in awe of the world. He'll keep you busy—and there will be more than a few sleepless nights. But the work you put in at the start, bonding with your puppy and teaching him well, will ultimately be more than worth it.

Photo Courtesy of
Joseph La Plante

*Photo Courtesy of Brenda Berardo*

# Final Preparations And Planning

With a dog as intelligent as a Rottie, you really need to be around for the whole first week and as much of the first month as possible, and that means taking time off work or negotiating to work at home during at least the first 24 hours, if not the first 48 hours. The more time you can dedicate in those first few days, the better for your new family member.

Start creating a list as you begin your search for a puppy or adult. You've already seen that there are a lot of preparations that need to be made, but preparing the house is just one of the important tasks. The following are some useful checklists to get you through the preparation for puppy and the aftermath of his arrival at your home.

## Puppy Supplies To Get Before Your Puppy Arrives

The following are essentials to have in place before your puppy arrives, to avoid having to run to the store in a panic when you realize you're missing something.

- Food
- Bed
- Crate
- Toys
- Water and food dishes
- Leash
- Collar
- Treats
- Training schedule and tools

All of these items should be set up and ready for use before the puppy arrives.

Photo Courtesy of
Debbie Diehl

## Pre-Arrival Home Inspection

No matter how busy you are, you need to take the time to inspect the home one more time before the puppy arrives. Set aside an hour or two to complete this a day or two before the puppy arrives.

## A Tentative Puppy Schedule

Prepare a tentative schedule to help you get started over the course of the week. Your days are about to get very busy, so you need somewhere to start before your puppy arrives. Use the information from Set a Schedule to get started, but make sure you do this earlier instead of later.

## Initial Meeting

Have a final meeting with all of the family members to make sure all of the rules discussed in Chapter 4 are remembered and understood before the puppy is a distraction. This includes how to handle the puppy. Determine who is going to be responsible for primary puppy care, including who will be the primary trainer. To help teach younger children about responsibility, a parent can pair with a child to manage the puppy's care. The child will be responsible for things like keeping the water bowl filled and feeding the puppy, and a parent can oversee the tasks.

Puppy training happens from the moment your Rottweiler is under your care. The rules and hierarchy should start to be established from that first car ride home. Even your kids will need to start making sure to establish themselves as higher up than the Rottie, though they won't need to be nearly as firm as the adults.

# The Ride Home

As tempting as it is to cuddle and try to make the ride comfortable, using a crate for the ride home is both safer and more comfortable for the puppy.

Before leaving, make sure you have everything you need prepared.

- The crate should be anchored with a cushion to make the trip safe.

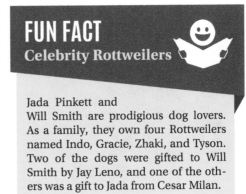

**FUN FACT**
**Celebrity Rottweilers**

Jada Pinkett and Will Smith are prodigious dog lovers. As a family, they own four Rottweilers named Indo, Gracie, Zhaki, and Tyson. Two of the dogs were gifted to Will Smith by Jay Leno, and one of the others was a gift to Jada from Cesar Milan.

*Photo Courtesy of*
*Teri Kenney*

- Call to make sure everything is still on schedule and make sure the puppy is ready.

- Ask, if you haven't already, if you can get the mother to leave her scent on a blanket to help make the puppy's transition more comfortable.

- Make sure your other adult remembers and will be on time to head to the pickup destination.

- If you have other dogs, make sure that all adults know what to do and where to go for that first neutral meeting.

Two adults should be present on the first trip. Ask the breeder if the puppy has been in a car before, and, if not, it is especially important to have someone who can give the puppy attention while the other person drives. The puppy will be in the crate, but someone can still provide comfort. It will definitely be scary because the puppy no longer has mom, siblings, or known people around, so having someone present to talk to the puppy will make it a little less of an ordeal for the little guy. Rottweilers may not be a fearful breed, but that doesn't mean they don't get scared when they are young.

This is the time to start teaching your puppy that car trips are enjoyable. This means making sure that the crate is secure instead of being loose to be moved around during the drive. You don't want to terrify the puppy by letting the crate slide around while the puppy is helpless inside. This kind of jostling will teach your canine that cars are terrifying instead of making them feel safe.

# First Night Frights

That first night is going to be scary to your little Rottweiler puppy. As understandable as this may be, there is only so much comfort you can give your new family member. Just like with a baby, the more you respond to cries and whimpering, the more you are teaching a puppy that negative behaviors will provide the desired results. You will need to be prepared for a balancing act to provide reassurance that things will be all right while keeping your puppy from learning that crying gets your attention.

Create a sleeping area just for your puppy near where you sleep. The area should have the puppy's bed tucked safely into a crate. It offers him a safe place to hide so that he can feel more comfortable in a strange new home. The entire area should be blocked off so that no one can get into it (and the puppy can't get out) during the night. It should also be close to

Photo Courtesy of
Chad Kerns

where people sleep so that the puppy doesn't feel abandoned. If you were able to get a blanket or pillow that smells like the mother, make sure this is in your puppy's space. Consider adding a little white noise to cover unfamiliar sounds that could scare your new pet.

Your puppy will make noises over the course of the night. Don't move the puppy away, even if the whimpering keeps you awake. If you give in, over time the whimpering, whining, and crying will get louder. Spare yourself the trouble later by teaching the puppy that it won't work. Being moved away from people will only scare the puppy more, reinforcing the anxiety. Over time, simply being close to you at night will be enough to reassure your puppy that everything will be all right.

Losing sleep is part of the deal of bringing a puppy into your home. Fortunately, it doesn't take as long to get a puppy acclimated as it takes with a human infant, so your normal schedule can resume more quickly.

Don't let your puppy into your bed that first night – or any other night – until he is fully housetrained. Once a Rottweiler learns that the bed is accessible, you can't train him not to hop on it. If he isn't housetrained, you'll need a new bed in the very near future.

Whatever housetraining path you use, you are going to need to keep to a schedule even during the night to train your puppy where to use the bathroom. Puppies will need to go to the bathroom every two to three hours, and you will need to get up during the night to make sure your puppy understands that he is to always go to the bathroom either outside or on the pee pad. If you let it go at night, you are going to have a difficult time training him that he cannot go in the house later.

# First Vet Visit

This is going to be a difficult task because you may feel a bit like you are betraying your puppy (especially with the looks your puppy will give you during shots and the following visits to the vet). However, it is necessary to do this within the first day or two of your puppy's arrival and may be required in the contract you signed with a breeder. You need to establish a baseline for the puppy's health so that the vet can track progress and monitor the puppy to ensure everything is going well as your Rottweiler develops and ages. It also creates a rapport between your Rottweiler and the vet, which can help too. The initial assessment gives you more information about your puppy, as well as giving you a chance to ask the vet questions and get advice.

It is certain to be an emotional trip for your Rottweiler, although it could be exciting in the beginning. Wanting to explore and greet everyone and everything is going to be something that your puppy is very likely to want to do. Both people and other pets are likely to attract your puppy's attention. This is a chance for you to work on socializing the puppy, though you will need to be careful. Always ask the person if it is all right for your puppy to meet any other pet, and wait for approval before letting your puppy move forward with meeting other animals. Pets at the vet's office are very likely to not be feeling great, which means they may not be very affable. You don't want a grumpy older dog or a sick animal to nip, hurt, or scare your puppy. Nor do you want your puppy to be exposed to anything potentially dangerous while still going through the shots. You want the other animal to be happy about the meeting (though not too excited) so that it is a positive experience for your puppy.

Having a positive first experience with other animals can make the visit to see the vet less of a scary experience, and something that your Rottweiler can enjoy, at least a little. This can help your puppy feel more at ease during the visits.

Depending on what the vet does during the first visit, you may want to be prepared to comfort your puppy. It probably won't involve shots, but even without them, vets can be overwhelming and scary for puppies. The first vet visit really should not include shots as your puppy is a new arrival, and shots will make your puppy feel less than comfortable.

If you already have a vet, take a few minutes to ask about their experience with the breed. Considering the reputation, some vets may not even want to have a Rottie in their waiting room. Since some people do not properly train Rotties, your vet may have had bad experiences that have tainted his or her opinion of the breed. Most of them realize the problem is with the people, not the dog, so find out how your vet feels before taking your pup for a first visit.

You want to find a vet that is fairly close to your home, usually within a few miles. If your puppy gets sick or injured, you want to be able to get to the vet quickly.

During the first visit, the vet will conduct an initial assessment of your Rottie – and it will be unpleasant for the puppy. The vet will be poking and pushing on the puppy, which can be incredibly jarring for a puppy who is not used to that. When the doctor does that to you, at least you understand what is going on – your puppy doesn't have a clue. Be ready to comfort your puppy and let the little pooch know that it is okay.

One of the most important things the vet will do is take your puppy's weight. This is something you are going to have to monitor for your Rottie's entire life because the breed is prone to obesity. Record the weight for yourself so you can see how quickly the puppy is growing. Ask your vet what a healthy weight is at each stage, and record that as well. Rottie should be growing unbelievably fast during that first year, but you should still make sure your Rottie isn't gaining more weight than is healthy.

The vet will give your puppy any shots that are due during that first visit as well. If this happens, be prepared for a day or two of your puppy feeling under the weather.

# The Start Of Training

As mentioned, training starts from the moment your Rottweiler becomes your responsibility, and that will be true for the entire life of your pooch. The breed's reputation for being easy to train is well earned, but it also means constant dedication. It will be the foundation for all of the training, so this is when you need to start taking a firm and consistent approach.

The focus during these first few weeks is to start housetraining and minimizing undesirable behavior, especially toward other animals and feelings of being territorial. Training from the start is vital, but don't take your new puppy to any classes just yet.

*Photo Courtesy of Francisco Bustamante*

Most puppies have not had all of the necessary shots, and good trainers will not allow them in classes until the full first round of shots is complete.

# CHAPTER 6.
# The First Month

The first week is definitely difficult, mostly because of how much work you will have to train your scared little Rottie. It will give you a fairly good understanding of your puppy's personality though, and that is something that you will be able to use to make it easier to both train your puppy and to figure out how best to keep the pup from getting bored. Lack of sleep will probably reduce how effective you will be in the early days, but as long as you stick to the rules, you will start seeing results much faster than with most other breeds since Rotties love to please.

With a week's worth of analyzing your puppy's personality, you will have a good idea of what kind of praise and attention work, as well as what treats get the best reactions. Incorporating what you have learned over that first month is going to prove to be a boon because as your Rottie starts to bond with you, that instinct to work with you is going to start to really show.

*Photo Courtesy of Jason Parnis*

# Not Up To Full Strength – Don't Overdo It In The First Month

Rottweilers may be known for their strength, but a puppy is nowhere near as strong as an adult. Watch for the telltale signs that he is tired, because like a human toddler, your pup is probably going to want to keep going even after he is past the point when he should be sleeping. He doesn't have quite as much energy as he thinks he does, so it is up to you to read the signs to know when to start calming him down and putting him to bed. You will need to be particularly aware of this during training. If your pup is too tired to learn, then he is going to be learning the wrong lessons during training. Be careful that you aren't pushing the training past the puppy's concentration threshold. When you start to see signs that your puppy is tiring too much to listen, go ahead and put the cutie to bed. Then you can get 40 winks without having to worry about your puppy being anxious or bored.

## FUN FACT
### Animal Activist and Rottweiler Owner

Leonardo DiCaprio is probably best known for his starring roles in a number of blockbuster films, but he is also an environmentalist and philanthropist. IFAW Animal Action Education, a component of the Leonardo DiCaprio Foundation, aims to educate and inspire young people to protect and preserve animals and the environment. In addition to the animal-loving efforts of his foundation, Mr. DiCaprio personally owns a Rottweiler named Baby.

Walks will be much shorter during that first month, and you won't be able to jog with your pup. When you do go out for walks, stay within a few blocks of home. You can do a bit of running on the leash in the yard if your puppy has a good bit of extra energy. This will help your Rottie learn how to behave on the leash. Don't worry – by the month's end, your puppy will have a lot more stamina so you can enjoy longer walks and short trips away from home if needed.

Even if your Rottweiler can't handle a long walk, you still need to make sure that the puppy gets adequate activity every day. Remember, he is from an intelligent breed, which means he will get in trouble when he gets bored – and if he has those habits as an adult, you will be in a lot of trouble trying to get him to stop those undesirable behaviors, like chewing on furniture and jumping on people when he is excited. Staying active will help him to not only be healthy, but also keep him mentally stimulated so that he is less likely to get in trouble around the home. You will quickly realize just how sedentary you have been if you have never had a dog before because you will be on the move almost all of the time the puppy is awake.

# Setting The Rules And Sticking To Them

*"As a puppy, you do not want to overdue exercise as this can sometimes lead to hip issues. Let them show you when they are tired and listen to their body and let them rest if they need it."*

**Maria Bledsoe**
*JeMar Rottweilers*

Rottweilers may want to please you, but your puppy has to know what the rules are. If you don't remain consistent, you are setting yourself and your Rottie up for a lot of contention since it will be difficult to convince your dog that you are serious. Your puppy is looking to you, so it is really all on you to keep that going.

*Photo Courtesy of Shawn Maguire*

A firm, consistent approach is best for both of you. You want to have fun together, but that also means making sure your Rottie knows that there are some things that are required. Given that Rottweilers have a long history of being protective, you have to make sure that your Rottie listens to you before reaching adulthood. Once your canine learns to listen to you, training your Rottie to do tricks can easily become a highlight to your day.

## Separation Anxiety

Rottweilers can get really attached to their people, which can lead to separation anxiety. This can be particularly true during the first month when your puppy is missing mommy. When worrying about when you will get home, your Rottie may decide to take out that anxiety on a host of items in your home, and a Rottweiler can do a lot of damage.

Photo Courtesy of
Robyn Zelden

In the beginning, keep the puppy's time alone to a minimum. The sounds of people around the house will help your Rottie understand that the separation is not permanent. After the first week or so, the alone time can involve you going out to get the mail, leaving the puppy inside alone for just a few minutes. You can then lengthen the amount of time you are away from the puppy over a few days until the puppy is alone for 30 minutes or so.

Here are some basic guidelines for when you start to leave your puppy alone.

- Take the Puppy Out About 30 Minutes Before You Leave.
- Tire The Puppy Out So That Your Leaving Is Not Such A Big Deal.
- Place The Puppy In The Puppy Area Well Ahead Of When You Go Out To Avoid Associating The Space With Something Bad Happening.
- Don't Give Your Puppy Extra Attention Right Before You Leave Because That Reinforces The Idea That You Give Attention Before Something Bad Happens.
- Avoid Reprimanding Your Rottie For Any Behavior While You Are Away. This Teaches Him To be more stressed because it will seem like you come home angry.

If your Rottie exhibits signs of separation anxiety, there are several things you can do to help make him comfortable during your absence.

- Chew toys can give your puppy something acceptable to gnaw on while you are away.
- A blanket or shirt that smells like you or other family members can help provide comfort too. Just make sure you don't give your puppy dirty clothing while you are away.
- Leave the area well lit, even if it is during the day. Should something happen and you get home later than intended, you don't want your Rottweiler to be in the dark.
- Turn on a stereo (classical music is best) or television (old-timey shows that don't have loud noises, like Mr. Ed or I Love Lucy) so that the house isn't completely quiet and unfamiliar noises are less obvious.

Since they are a smart breed, it is not going to take your Rottie long to notice the kind of behaviors that indicate you are leaving. Grabbing your keys, purse, wallet, and other indications will quickly become triggers that can make your Rottie anxious. Don't make a big deal out of it. If you act normal, over time this will help your Rottie to understand that your leaving is fine and that everything will be all right.

*Photo Courtesy of Danni Chapman*

# Training Areas To Start During The First Month

Training is covered in a later chapter, but there are several critical aspects that you will need to start during the first month:

- Housetraining

- Crate training

- Chewing

- Barking

- Protection (you won't start this during the first month, but you will need to start gauging for it if you want your dog to be an ideal protector)

You need to find out how much the breeder did in housetraining and other areas. The best trainers may even have puppies listening to one or two commands before they go home with you. If this is the case (and it is easier to do with Rotties), you will want to keep using those commands with your puppy so that the training is not lost. This can help you establish the right tone to use as the puppy will already know what the words mean and how to react to them. Once he understands that, he will more quickly pick up on other uses of that tone as the way you talk when you are training. It is another great way to let your little love know when you mean business versus when you want to play. These kinds of distinctions are easily picked up by Rottweilers and he will be more than happy to oblige.

# CHAPTER 7.
# Housetraining

*"I like dogs. You always know what a dog is thinking. It has four moods: happy, sad, cross, and concentrating. Also, dogs are faithful, and they do not tell us lies because they cannot talk."*

Mark Haddon,
*The Curious Incident of the Dog in the Night-Time*

If you decide to adopt a puppy, you are going to have to housetrain the little guy (it is one reason some people won't adopt a puppy, no matter how cute). Other kinds of training may be easy for Rotties, but housetraining is a unique challenge for every breed. You are going to have to be patient to get the point of the training through to your buddy because it is not natural to hold it until there is an acceptable place and time. Even humans have a difficult time learning, and they only have to go to specific rooms in the house. You are trying to get your puppy to go outside and do his business, and you pretty much have to be there monitoring the progress during the first few months (even if you have a yard). This is why it is so important to set a schedule and then not deviate from it.

Using a leash can be very helpful in ensuring that your puppy learns when and where to go, but there will still be challenges as you work to establish the hierarchy and convince your puppy to listen to you.

Two rules should be followed during this time.

1. Your puppy is not to be left free to roam the house alone. Your Rottie won't be pleased with the idea of being in a soiled crate, so that is a deterrent from using the bathroom when you are not around.

2. Your puppy should have constant, easy access to the locations where you plan to housetrain him. If you can't provide this, you will need to have frequent trips outside as your puppy learns where to do his business. This is the best way to train a puppy to go outside, and a leash can help you combine housetraining with leash training (although this could make it a little more difficult).

Start with a training plan, then make sure that you are as strict with yourself as you are with your puppy Or, actually, be even more firm with yourself. You are the key to the puppy learning to go in the spots you want used for this particularly difficult aspect of training your companion. To make this plan work, you need to make some decisions before the puppy arrives so that you can best prepare for this difficult training.

# Inside Or Outside – Potty Training Options

Something that you have on your side when it comes to training is that your Rottweiler is going to want the praise that comes with the act of using the bathroom outside. They tend to pick up the idea a bit faster than many other breeds. Once a Rottie understands to use the bathroom outside, you won't have to be as wary of him going inside as long as you keep a schedule and get him outside on that schedule.

If your breeder has already started housetraining your dog, stick to that method. Changing it will make your Rottie more likely to either get confused or to believe that housetraining is optional.

*Photo Courtesy of Craig Kappen*

## Your Housetraining Options And Considerations

*"Use a crate! Be consistent and NEVER leave the dog unattended in a section of the house. If training to potty indoors set up a secure area you can leave the puppy where it is okay to potty, preferably not on the floor that looks exactly like the rest of your house."*

**Teresa Bradley**
*Neu-Rodes Rottweilers*

Here are your options when it comes to housetraining your puppy:

- Pee pads – you should have several around the home for training
- Regular outings outside – set the schedule based on your puppy's sleeping and eating schedule
- Rewards – this can be treats in the beginning, but should quickly shift to praise

There are several factors that will influence how you begin training, particularly the weather outside. If the weather is too cold or hot, stick with training your puppy inside. He will not be likely to focus if he is too uncomfortable. If your puppy associates going to the bathroom with discomfort, he is going to be much more stubborn than if he is able to relieve himself inside where it is more comfortable.

Photo Courtesy of Karen Smith

In the beginning the best way to housetrain is by going out a lot of times, including at night, so that your puppy learns to keep all business outside. During the first few months, it is best to use a leash when you take the puppy out. This allows you to help him learn to walk on a leash and keeps him from getting distracted.

## Setting A Schedule And Outdoor Restroom Location

*"Find a suitable spot in your yard and always take the puppy to that spot. Wait until the job is done and then have a big celebration with lots of treats. Never leave the puppy unsupervised in the house out of its crate. If the puppy starts to potty, immediately pick up and take outside. "*

**Kathryn Lovan**
*Halo Rottweilers*

Those early days are going to be difficult. You need to keep an eye on your puppy and have housetraining sessions after several key activities:

- After eating
- After waking up from sleeping or naps
- On a schedule (after it has been established)

Watch your Rottweiler for cues and to determine what activities make the little pup have to go. This includes things like sniffing and circling, two very common activities as a puppy searches for a place to go. Start tailoring your schedule around your puppy's unique needs.

Puppies have small bladders and little control in the early days. If you have to train your pup to go inside, there needs to be a single designated space with a clean pee pad in the puppy area, and you need to stock up on the appropriate pads for the puppy to have somewhere to go that isn't the floor. The pads are better than newspaper and can absorb more. You will need to plan to transition as quickly as possible before the Rottweiler learns that going inside is acceptable – this will be incredibly difficult to retrain later if you let him go inside for too long, particularly as he realizes that it is easier to go inside.

A designated restroom space can help make the experience easier. The Rottweiler will begin to associate one area of the yard for one purpose. When you get there, the expectation will be easier to understand faster than if you let the puppy sniff around and go anywhere in the yard. Having him go to one spot regularly will not only make training easier, but cleanup will be much simpler too; that way you can continue to use the whole yard instead of having to worry about stepping in waste whenever you or anyone else goes outside.

When out for walks is the perfect time to train your puppy to go. Between walks and the yard, your puppy will come to see the leash as a sign

Photo Courtesy of Gillian Hall

that it is time to relieve the bladder, which could become a Pavlovian response. Given that Rotties are so smart, it won't take your companion long to understand the correlation either.

## Key Words

*"Use a command to teach the dog to relieve themselves and when you get the desired behavior, reward the behavior verbally and with food or a toy."*

**Daviann Mitchell**
*Nighthawk Rottweilers*

All training should include key words, even housetraining. You and all members of the family should know what words to use when training your dog where to go to the bathroom, and you should all be using those words consistently. If you have paired an adult with a child, the adult should be the one using the keyword during training.

Be careful not to select words that you often use inside the home because you don't want to confuse your puppy. Selecting the right word is a lot trickier than you might think because you use some of the words in conversation more often than you might expect (particularly if you are potty training a child at the same time). Plan to use something like "Get busy" to let your puppy know it's time to get to work. It's not a phrase most people use in their daily routine, so not something you are likely to say when you don't mean for your puppy to use the bathroom.

# Positive Reinforcement – Rewarding Good Behavior

Positive reinforcement is unbelievably effective with Rottweilers, even the puppies. In the beginning, take a few pieces of kibble with you when you are teaching your puppy where to go, both inside and outside. Learning that you are the one in charge will help teach the Rottie to look to you for cues and instructions.

While you are being firm and consistent, when your puppy does the right thing you have to lavish the little pup with praise. If you gently lead your puppy to the area on a leash without any other stops, it will become obvious over time that your Rottweiler should go there to use the bathroom. Once

*Photo Courtesy of Francisco Bustamante*

you get outside, encourage your Rottweiler to go once you get to the place in the yard where you want him to go. In the beginning, this probably won't take too long, and as soon as he does his business, give him immediate and very enthusiastic praise. Pet your puppy as you talk to let the little guy know just how good the action was. Once the praise is done, return back inside immediately. This is not playtime, so do not remain outside. You want your puppy to associate certain outings as designated potty time.

Praise is far more effective for Rotties, but you can give your puppy a treat after a few successful trips outside. Definitely do not make treats a habit after each trip because you do not want your Rottweiler to expect it every time. The last thing you want is for your Rottie to learn that this is all about treats. The lesson is to go outside, and that may include treats when it is done consistently.

The best way to train in that first month or two is to go out every hour or two, even at night. You will need to set an alarm to wake you within that time to take the puppy outside. Use the leash to keep the focus on using the bathroom, give the same enthusiastic praise, then immediately return inside and go to bed. It is incredibly difficult, but your Rottie will get the hang of it a lot faster if there really isn't a long period between potty breaks. Over time, the pup will need to go out less frequently, giving you more rest.

If your Rottie has an accident, it is important to refrain from punishing the puppy. Accidents are not a reason to punish a puppy – it really reflects more on your training and schedule than what the puppy has learned. That said, accidents are pretty much an inevitability. When it happens, tell your puppy, "No. Potty outside!" and clean the mess immediately. Once that is done take the puppy outside to go. Of course, if your puppy doesn't go, he doesn't get any praise.

# CHAPTER 8.
# Socialization And Experience

*"You have to socialize these pups early on. Between the ages of 9 weeks to 16 weeks is the most crucial time frame to get started with socializing. I know what people are thinking, that is the time that they can contract parvo, but there is a way to do this without putting your puppy in danger. Go to a friend's house that has safe dogs or downtown to an area where dogs don't go but they can meet people."*

**Bobby and Melissa Kemp**
*Gold Hill Kennels*

Photo Courtesy of
Christina Mckibbin

Photo Courtesy of
Christine Hostetter

Rottweilers are absolutely unafraid and their desire to protect their pack is what makes them such great guard dogs. However, as a member of your family, you want your Rottie to be happy around other people and dogs because the vast majority of them are no threat at all. Socialization allows your Rottweiler puppy to learn that it can be a lot of fun to play with people you invite into your home and dogs that you encounter out on your walks. To teach your Rottie that the world is actually something to enjoy and not something to be constantly wary of, you have to plan to start socialization from a very early age. Your puppy will need to have all of the necessary vaccinations before being exposed to other dogs, but that happens fairly early in your puppy's life.

81

# Socialization Is Critical For Rottweilers

*"Socializing must be positive and constant for the first 3 YEARS of your Rottweiler's life. They are not supposed to trust things naturally, they must be taught."*

**Elissa O'Sullivan**
*Falkore Rottweilers*

Socialization is important for all dogs, but for all guard dog breeds, like the Rottweiler, German Shepherd, and Doberman Pinscher, it is absolutely critical. While the reputation of the Rottweiler is decidedly undeserved – they are every bit as cuddly and loving as a Lab or Collie – they do have a tendency to be wary of strangers and other animals. Failing to socialize your Rottie can result in a dangerous adult dog. Most Rottweilers that aren't properly socialized will want to dominate other dogs. They aren't seeking to fight the dogs they encounter, but they want the other dogs to know that they are the boss.

*Photo Courtesy of Linn Amalie Brekke*

The benefit of early socialization is that it can make things that much more enjoyable for everyone involved, no matter what the situation is. A socialized dog will approach the world from a much better place than a dog that is not socialized. All other rules still apply during socialization, so keep that in mind while you help your dog meet new friends.

Photo Courtesy of
Sandy Harrell

# Properly Greeting New People

Greeting new people is usually a pretty easy task outside of the home, but it can be a bit tricky when you are at home. Training your Rottie how to treat visitors may take a little longer because he may not want a lot of attention – or he might. Rottweilers are all unique. Some prefer to analyze visitors before deciding to interact; they love their people, seeing visitors as more of a disruption from pack time. Others will see you enjoying the inter-action and will want to be a part of it. Either attitude is perfectly fine, as long as your Rottie learns that the people you invite into your home are all right.

1. Try to have your puppy meet new people daily, if possible. This could be during walks or other activities where you get out of the house. If you can't meet new people daily, try for at least 4 times a week.

2. Invite friends and family over, and let them spend a few minutes just giving the puppy attention. If your puppy has a favorite game or activi-ty, let them know so that they can play with the puppy. This will win the little guy over very quickly.

3. Once your puppy is old enough to learn tricks (after the first month – don't try to teach tricks in the beginning), demonstrate the tricks for vis-itors who are wary of your puppy. This will be really important as your

## FUN FACT
### German Origins

Rottweil is a town in Baden-Württemberg in southwest Germany. Rottweiler dogs supposedly derive their name from this town and were historically used by butchers in the region to herd livestock and pull meat carts to market. These dogs were known in German as Rottweiler Metzgerhund, which translates to 'Rottweil butcher's dog.'

puppy gets bigger because a lot of people are nervous around Rotties. This helps them see that your dog is just as clownish and playful as many of the other large breeds.

4.      Avoid crowds for the first few months. When your puppy is several months to a year old, though, try to go to dog-friendly events so that your pup can learn not to be uncomfortable around a large group of people.

## Behavior Around Other Dogs

*"Introduce your Rottweiler to all species of animals and do not allow any aggression. Recognize not all Rottweilers are suited to live in a multi species family and don't risk your dog or someone else's pet attempting to force a friendship. Co existence is ok, as long as it is safe for all involved."*

**Daviann Mitchell**
*Nighthawk Rottweilers*

Photo Courtesy of Kerry Lowe

Once your puppy has had all of the vaccinations, you can start having friends and family with friendly dogs come over for a play date. Romping around the home with another dog can teach your Rottie that dogs can play in a way that people can't. By inviting over friends and family who have well-behaved and friendly dogs of all sizes, you can make socialization much easier in the early days.

When going for walks, you may want to be a little more cautious because you won't be as familiar with all of the dogs you meet. You don't want your puppy to try to meet an old dog that isn't feeling well or a dog that is not properly socialized because these kinds of interactions can teach your Rottie to be suspicious and wary when out walking.

You always need to ask the owners before interacting with another dog you don't know. People with less sociable dogs or older dogs will let you know if their dog isn't sociable, so you can walk on, keeping your puppy on the opposite side of your body from the less friendly dog. This is part of leash training too, but it is far more critical with a large dog like a Rottweiler.

Dog parks can be very tricky for Rottweilers, even when they are well socialized. First, you have to make sure that the off-leash area allows for the breed. Then you have to contend with the apprehension of the people at the park. And Rotties are not great at putting up with dogs at the park that are careless or aggressive. Your Rottie may snap at an obnoxious dog or one that is constantly trying to show domination – this is a breed that really does not put up with that kind of nonsense. Go to the park when there are only a couple of dogs around so you can ensure that your Rottie remains comfortable and that there aren't any ill-behaved dogs that will make it a miserable experience for everyone. Rottweilers rarely start fights, but they have no problem ending them. Because of this, dog parks usually aren't a great place for breeds like the Rottweiler, mostly because other people simply fail to train their dogs properly.

## CHAPTER 9.
# Living With Other Dogs

While you always have to plan the first introduction of a new dog, there are many considerations that have to be made for breeds like the Rottweiler. Puppies will be easier to introduce than adult dogs (if you decide to rescue a Rottie, it is generally recommended that you not have other dogs), but that doesn't mean that you won't have any issues. Rottweilers don't tend to like other dogs. Puppies may not have the same kind of bias quite yet, but there is still a lot of work to be done. On the plus side, having a dog already in your home can help your puppy become socialized earlier. If your current dog or dogs have any undesirable behaviors, you may want to try to work those out before your puppy arrives too – you don't want your Rottie learning bad habits.

*Photo Courtesy of*
*Megan Bartz-Offord*

Photo Courtesy of
Genesis Perez

# Introducing Your New Puppy

*"As a small puppy never allow it to torment an older dog. If you have other pets you need to know their tolerance. I start by holding the puppy while they sniff the puppy and then I make it very clear the puppy is MINE, and then I slowly introduce it to each pet one at a time."*

**Kathryn Lovan**
*Halo Rottweilers*

Always introduce new dogs – even puppies – in a neutral place away from your home. Even if you have never had problems with your current dog (or dogs), you are about to change their world. Select a park or other area where your dog will not feel territorial and plan to introduce your dog to the puppy there. This gives the animals the opportunity to meet and get to know each other before entering your home together.

When introduce your dog and puppy, make sure you have at least one other adult with you so there's a person to manage each canine. If you have more than one dog, then you should have one adult per dog. This will make

Photo Courtesy of
Abby Jane Veit

it easier to keep all of the dogs under control. Even the best dogs can get overly excited about meeting a puppy. One of the people who needs to be there is the person who is in charge in the home (or people if you have more than one person in charge). This helps establish the pack hierarchy.

Don't hold onto your puppy when the dogs meet. While you may want to protect the puppy and make him feel comfortable by holding him, it has the opposite effect. Your puppy will likely feel trapped, with no way to escape. Being on the ground means that the puppy can run if he feels the need. Stand near the puppy with your feet a little bit a part. That way if the puppy decides to escape from your dog, he can quickly hide behind your legs.

Watch for raised hackles on your dog. The puppy and each dog should have a few minutes to sniff each other, making sure that there is always slack in the leash. This helps them feel more relaxed since they won't feel like you are trying to restrain them. Your dog will likely either want to play or will simply ignore the puppy.

- If they want to play, just be careful that the dog doesn't accidentally hurt the puppy.

- If the dog ends up ignoring the puppy after an initial sniff, that is fine too.

If your dog's hackles are up or if your dog is clearly unhappy, keep them apart until your dog seems more comfortable.

Don't force the meeting.

The introduction could take a while, depending on individual dog personalities. The friendlier and more accepting your dog is, the easier it will be to incorporate your new puppy into the home. For some dogs a week is enough time to start feeling comfortable together. For other dogs, it could take a couple of months before they are fully accepting of the new puppy. Since this is a completely new dynamic in your household, your current dog may not be pleased with you bringing a little bundle of energy into his daily life. This is enough to make anyone unhappy, but especially a dog that has grown accustomed to a certain lifestyle. The older your dog is, the more likely it is that a puppy will be an unwelcome addition. Older dogs can get cranky around puppies that don't understand the rules or don't seem to know when enough is enough. The goal is to make your puppy feel welcome and safe, while letting your older dog know that your love is just as strong as ever.

Once your new family member and the rest of the canine pack start to get acquainted and feel comfortable with each other, you can head home. As they enter the house, they will have a bit more familiarity with each other, making your current dogs feel more comfortable with the new addition to the family.

Once home, take the dogs into the yard and remove the leashes. You will need one adult per dog, including the puppy. If they seem to be all right or the dog is indifferent to the puppy, you can let your dog inside, releash the puppy, and keep the puppy on the leash as you go inside.

Put the puppy in the puppy area when the introductions are done.

*Photo Courtesy of John Thomas*

# Introducing An Adult Rottie

If a rescue does not know how much socialization an adult Rottweiler has been through and can't say how well the Rottie has gotten along with other dogs, it's best not to adopt that particular adult Rottweiler. They are a fantastic breed, but since they are prone to disliking their own species, you don't want to have to return the rescue because of issues with your current dog.

Even if the rescue knows that the Rottie is fine with other dogs, you have to approach the introduction and first few weeks (and probably months) with caution. The new Rottie will need his own stuff in the beginning, and should be kept in a separate area when you aren't around until you know that there won't be any fighting.

Plan for the introduction to take at least an hour. It probably won't take that long, but you must make sure that all of the dogs are comfortable during the introduction. Since the dogs are all adults, they will need to move at their own pace, and for Rottweilers meeting new dogs, this may take a little while.

Photo Courtesy of Skylor Cash

Follow the same steps to introduce your current dogs with your new dog as you would with a puppy.

- Start on neutral territory.

- Have one adult human per dog present at the introduction (this is even more important when introducing an adult).

- Introduce one dog at a time – don't let several dogs meet your new Rottie at one time. Having multiple dogs approaching at once in an unfamiliar environment with people the Rottie doesn't know very well – you can probably see how this can be nerve-racking for any new dog.

Unlike with a puppy, make sure to bring treats to the meeting of two adults dogs. The animals will respond well to the treats, and you will have a way to quickly distract all of the dogs if they are too tense with each other.

During the introduction, watch the Rottie and your dogs to see if they raise their hackles. This is one of the first really obvious signs that a dog is uncomfortable. If the Rottie's hackles are up, back off the introductions for a little bit. Do this by calling your current dog back first. This is also when you should start waving treats. Avoid pulling on the leashes to separate them. You don't want to add physical tension to the situation because that could trigger a fight. Treats will work for all dogs present in the beginning, and your other dogs should be able to respond to your calling their names.

If any of the dogs are showing their teeth or growling, call your dog back and give the dogs a chance to settle down first. Use the treats and a calming voice to get them to relax. Let them start to initiate interest in each other. You want them all to feel comfortable during the first meeting, so you can't force the friendship. If they seem uncomfortable or wary at first, you will need to let them move at their own pace.

# Establishing The New Norm

The sense of familiarity established during the first meeting doesn't mean that the dogs will have automatically bonded, so there may be some tension, especially early on. This is why it is important to keep them separated in the home, particularly when you're away. The puppy should be in his designated area, to make it easier for him to relax and start to get familiar with the new environment.

Make sure that none of your other dog's stuff ends up in the puppy's area. When the puppy invariably chews on everything he can reach, this can be seen by your dog as a threat to his place in the pack and will generate unnecessary tension. Before letting your puppy out of his designated area, make sure to do a bit of cleanup around the house and store your older dog's toys in a safe place.

Mealtime is another potential problem time, so you should feed your puppy in a different location, at least in the beginning. Food tends to be the source of most dog fights. As your puppy gets older, you can start to feed him with your other dogs, but still keep them separated.

Your current dog probably isn't going to be happy about sharing you with the puppy. Schedule one-on-one time with your dog, including longer walks, extra training, or general play. This will let your dog know that the

*Photo Courtesy of
Tonya Renee Jones
Lakeview Kennel*

puppy is not a replacement. You should start keeping a schedule with your dog so that you don't change the amount of time you spend together after the puppy arrives. It also means you will need to be just as firm and consistent with your puppy as you are with your dog. If you are more lenient with your puppy, this will create tension.

There are a number of benefits to having a dog in the home that already knows the rules. The biggest is that your dog will reprimand your puppy for misbehavior and help him learn his place in the pack. Of course, your dog can't be the primary trainer, but it's nice to have someone helping reinforce the rules. As long as your dog is gentle, let him discipline the puppy – just make sure there isn't too much aggression or roughness to the behavior correction. Should your dog opt out of this role, that's fine. It's best to let your dog decide what kind of relationship he wants to have with the puppy.

Once your Rottie accepts your other dogs (and vice versa), he will be as protective of your dogs as he is of you. This can be wonderfully entertaining, particularly if you have bigger dogs. It is nearly certain that your Rottie is going to be the most outgoing of the bunch, and that can lead to some very interesting encounters. Being smart, your Rottweiler will quickly learn when to step up for your dogs, and with proper socialization, that will not be often, making your trips outside enjoyable.

# Biting, Fighting, And Puppy Anger Management With Multiple Rottie Puppies

*"As a small puppy never allow it to torment an older dog. If you have other pets you need to know their tolerance. I start by holding the puppy while they sniff the puppy and then I make it very clear the puppy is MINE, and then I slowly introduce it to each pet one at a time."*

*Kathryn Lovan*
*Halo Rottweilers*

Given how big your puppy is going to get, you definitely have to be firm in the early days, making sure that he learns not to bite anyone (including animals) from a very early age. Adopting more than one puppy at a time is at least twice as much work. If you want to raise more than one Rottweiler puppy at one time, you are in for a real challenge. They are going to want to please you and spend time with you, but they will have the same energy level, which means that their misbehaviors can feed off each other. It will take a lot more energy and work to make sure they behave appropriately.

Be prepared to lose your personal life, particularly your social life, if you have more than one puppy at a time. Taking care of those little puppies is going to be like having two full-time jobs. First, you must spend time with them both, together and separately. This means spending twice as much time with the puppies, making sure they get along well, learn at an even pace, and still get to have designated time with you. Each puppy will have its own strengths and weaknesses, and you need to learn what those are for each one, as well as learning how well the puppies work together. If they both behave during alone time with you, but tend to misbehave or fail to listen when they are together, you will need to adjust your approach to make sure they both understand the rules. This is a real challenge, especially if they whine when you're playing with one of them and not the other (which is very likely with Rottweilers).

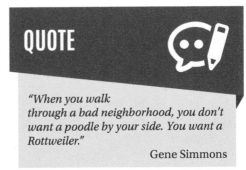

QUOTE

*"When you walk through a bad neighborhood, you don't want a poodle by your side. You want a Rottweiler."*

Gene Simmons

Photo Courtesy of
Bobbi Lambier

You can always have someone else play or train with one puppy while you do the same with the other, then switch puppies. This builds bonds while letting the puppies know that they both have to listen to you and your training partner. Both puppies will also be happily occupied, so they won't be whimpering or feeling lonely while you're playing with the other puppy.

There may be some fighting between the puppies and you need to stop that immediately. Over time, you should be able to work out any aggressive behavior as long as you are consistent from the beginning. As long as they understand the rules and abide by them, your Rotties likely won't give you too much trouble.

# Older Dogs And Your Rottie Puppy

If your dog is older, keep in mind that puppies are energetic and likely to keep trying to engage the older dog in play. This can be incredibly trying for your older pup, which is something you definitely need to keep in mind when your puppy and your dog interact. Make sure that your older canine isn't getting too tired of the puppy's antics because you don't want your puppy to learn to snap at other dogs. Watch for signs that your older dog is ready for some alone time, some time alone with you, or just a break from the puppy.

Once your Rottie is ready to leave the puppy area for good, you will still want to make sure that your older dog has safe places to go to be alone in case he or she just doesn't feel up to being around a spry young thing. This will reduce the likelihood that your puppy will get repeatedly scolded and therefore learn to be wary of older dogs.

# CHAPTER 10.
# Training Your Rottweiler Puppy

*"The Rottweiler wants to please you. Right from day one when you bring your puppy home, it's important to start training immediately. They need to know what is expected of them, incorporate training into their play time, teaching them to work for their reward."*

**Deborah Bram**
*Flusstal Rottweilers*

## HELPFUL TIP
### ARC Pet Therapy Program

Therapy dogs are dogs who volunteer with their owners in places such as schools, nursing homes, and hospitals. Unlike service dogs who are trained to perform specific tasks for disabled persons, therapy dogs provide comfort and enrichment to the lives of children, seniors, and many others. The American Rottweiler Club (ARC) Pet Therapy Program aims to combat the stigma surrounding the Rottweiler breed by bringing volunteer therapy dogs into community settings and demonstrating the calm and loving side of this breed. For more information about therapy dog training programs, visit the American Kennel Club's Therapy Dog Training webpage.
References:
https://www.akc.org/sports/title-recognition-program/therapy-dog-program/
https://www.amrottclub.org/work-and-play/therapy-dog/

One of the reasons that people adopt Rotties is because of how easy they are to train. Almost from the beginning, praise works as well (and soon better) than treats. Their intelligence means that they quickly figure out what commands mean and their desire to please means that they unlikely to ignore commands that they know well. While Rotties need to know that you are in control, you will almost certainly be spared the kind of fight you have with most intelligent dogs (including German Shepherds). Rotties can be stubborn, but they are also far easier to persuade to do things your way than most large intelligent dogs. They are more interested in working with you than in trying to get their way.

Working with a smart, energetic puppy can be tiring – even when he wants to work with you. Puppies simply can't focus the way adult dogs do. There is just too much distraction and things to explore as a puppy. By making sure to follow through with a few actions, you will find that your Rottweiler will pick up on the training much quicker. Keep in mind that training your puppy is a long-term commitment. Even if your Rottweiler isn't rebellious, the puppy probably just wants to have fun. Your puppy won't want to anger you, but gentle begging and puppy eyes can be very effective against all but the most determined parent, and Rottweilers will learn that, particularly if you give in during a training session.

Photo Courtesy of Rachel Labidi

# Firm And Consistent

There are many times in training where you will feel something is close enough. This is never a good idea with intelligent dogs. They study their people and figure out ways to get what they want with as little work as possible. Wanting to please you will still motivate a Rottweiler, but if you are willing to give an inch, he will take it and then see how much further you can be pushed. Exceptions and leniency are seen by your puppy as having some control over the situation, and that makes it much harder for him to take you seriously.

Keeping a consistent and firm approach during training will make life far easier for you and your puppy. Even if you are tired at the end of a long day at work, you have to enforce the rules. If you don't feel up to it, have a family member do the training. If you don't have anyone to help you, you can change up the training a bit to make it more enjoyable. It's fine to change things up if you are having a rough time, as long as you remain consistent. Consistency and firmness do not mean that you have to do the same thing all of the time. You just need to make sure that your puppy understands that you are in charge and there is no negotiating on that. This will keep your puppy on the right track to being a great companion instead of a dictator.

# Gain Respect Early

*"A Rottweiler puppy will 'test' the new owner by growling at them, the pup must be corrected as this is not allowed. A Rottweiler puppy needs to know who is in charge."*

**Grace Acosta**
*Acosta Rottweilers*

Being firm and consistent in your approach to training will start gaining you respect from your young canine early in your relationship. Positive reinforcement is the best way to gain respect, particularly if you use positive interaction. Playing with and training your puppy every day helps build a healthy, positive relationship that will teach your puppy where he or she fits into the pack. Your puppy learns that it is part of the family, but that you are the one in charge.

# Operant Conditioning Basics

Photo Courtesy of Amy Greenall

Operant conditioning is the scientific term for actions and consequences. You must provide your Rottweiler puppy with the right consequences for each behavior.

The best way to use operant conditioning is through positive reinforcement, particularly since Rottweilers are so attached to people. This type of training is more effective with working dogs and dogs that have a long history with people. They want to work with you and fulfill their tasks. Knowing that they are doing something right does a lot more to encourage their behavior than knowing when they do something wrong. They will keep trying until they get it right.

There are two types of reinforcements for operant conditioning:

- Primary reinforcements
- Secondary reinforcements

You will use both during your Rottweiler training.

# Primary Reinforcements

A primary reinforcement gives your dog something that he needs to survive, like food or social interaction. Initially, you will rely on primary reinforcements since you don't have to teach your Rottie to enjoy them. However, you have to keep a balance. Mealtime and playtime should never be denied to your puppy, no matter how poorly he performs. These things are essential to living, and are nonnegotiable. It is things like treats and extra playtime that you use to reinforce good behavior.

Err on the side of providing too much affection over too many treats. If you rely on treats instead of attention, you are setting yourself and your pup up for serious health problems later.

Photo Courtesy of
Debbie Bram
Flusstal Rottweilers

# Secondary Reinforcements

Without a doubt, Pavlov's experiment with dogs is the most recogniz-able example of secondary reinforcement. Pavlov taught test dogs to asso-ciate the ringing of a bell to mealtime. They were conditioned to associate something with a primary reinforcement. You can see this in your home when you use a can opener. If you have any cats or dogs, they probably come running as soon as the can opener starts going.

Secondary reinforcements work because your Rottweiler will associate the trigger with something that is required. This makes your puppy more likely to do as he is told. Dogs that are taught to sit using a treat only will au-tomatically react by sitting down when you have a treat in your hand. They won't even wait for you to tell them to sit. They know that sitting means more food, so they automatically do it once you make that association. Of course, this is not proper training because they need to learn to sit when you say sit, and not just when you have a treat. That is the real challenge.

Fortunately, it is relatively easy to train Rottweiler puppies with the right trigger because they are both intelligent and eager to please. While they may enjoy food, you can show them that the trigger is a word, not food. They will get it much faster than many other dog breeds.

You can also use toys and attention as a way of getting your Rottweiler to do the right thing. If you have a regular schedule and you are willing to change it a little to give your puppy a little extra attention for doing something right, that will be just as effective as a treat. You can take the pup on an extra walk, spend a little more time playing with a favorite toy, or take some time to cuddle.

Sometimes punishment is required too, but you need to be very careful about how you do it. Trying to punish a Rottweiler can be tricky, but denying your Rott-weiler attention can work very well. Simply put your puppy in a penned off area where he can see you but cannot interact with you. The little guy will whine and whimper to let you know that he wants out. Don't give in. Just ignore your puppy for as long as the pup makes noise to teach the lesson about proper behavior.

Punishments must happen right after the event. If your Rottweiler chews something up and you don't find out for several hours, it's too late to punish the puppy. The same is true for rewards. To reinforce behavior, the reward or punishment must be almost immediate. When you praise or punish your puppy, make sure you keep eye contact. You can also take the puppy by the scruff of the neck to ensure that you keep eye contact. You won't need to do that when you're praising your pooch because he will automatically keep eye contact. Rotties can be absolutely driven by hearing your praise.

Photo Courtesy of
Megan Bartz-Offord

# Why Food Is A Bad Reinforcement Tool

Treats should be used in the early stages when your puppy has not been conditioned to respond to secondary reinforcements. This will give you something to help your puppy learn to focus as you train the puppy to understand other incentives. It should not take too long before you can start transitioning away from treats as a reinforcement tool. Treats are also the best way of training certain types of behavior, such as rolling over. Your puppy will automatically follow the treat, making it easy to understand what you mean with your command. They cannot handle a lot of additional weight, so you'll need to find other incentives that work better. Use treats sparingly.

Another reason to use treats sparingly is because you don't want your puppy to respond to you primarily when you have food. If your Rottweiler associates training with treats, you may have a difficult time training your puppy to listen to you without them.

Treats can be used in the early stages when your puppy's metabolism is high and has not been conditioned to respond to secondary reinforcements. This will give you something to help your puppy learn to focus as you train the puppy to understand other incentives. It should not take too long before you can start transitioning away from treats as a reinforcement tool.

Treats are best for the beginning commands (sit, stay, and leave it). Your dog does not understand words yet, and will quickly make the connection between what you are saying and why the treat is being offered. Treats are also the best way of training certain types of behavior, such as rolling over. Your puppy will automatically follow the treat, making it easy to understand what you mean. Leave it is very difficult to teach without treats because there is no incentive to drop something if your puppy really wants the object already in his or her mouth. Treats are something that will make the puppy drop whatever is in the puppy's mouth as the attention and desire focuses on food. Once your puppy understands Leave it, you really should not use treats for training.

# Small Steps To Success

The first few weeks, or maybe even the first couple of months, with your puppy are a time with a very steep learning curve. The best way to train the puppy is to realize that you need to start slow – don't begin with expectations that your puppy will be housetrained in a week (that won't happen). Your puppy must learn the daily routine. Once the schedule and environment are less new and exciting, your Rottie will have an easier time focusing during training sessions.

Training should begin from day 1. Even though your puppy is just getting to know the environment, you need to start putting some rules in place. As your puppy gets familiar with you and the environment, you can teach your Rottweiler about his area and crate for sleeping. Learning to go into the crate on command has some obvious benefits, particularly if you leave home every day. Use treats to train the puppy to go into the crate and do other basic activities.

Starting from day 1 doesn't mean trying to do everything at once– you must start small. Give treats for little things that your puppy might do anyway, like exploring the crate. Once your Rottweiler starts to understand the reward system, training will get easier.

# Basic Behavior Training

*""The first few days the puppy will experience separation anxiety from being away from the litter, so it's important to work thru that immediately, start crate training and house breaking as soon as possible. As the puppy settles in, they think you are its litter mate, the biting of the hands begin, nipping, trying to become dominant. It's important that you nip these behaviors immediately and continue to reinforce correct behavior as the puppy grows"*

**Deborah Bram**
*Flusstal Rottweilers*

The next chapter covers basic command training, but it's different than training your Rottie in different types of behavior. Soon after your puppy arrives, you need to start training out the bad behaviors, and that is not

*Photo Courtesy of Heather Jones*

restricted to just training sessions. It's something you need to constantly teach your puppy over the course of the day.

## Chewing And Nipping

Chewing and nipping are behaviors you want to stop as soon as possible because it will be much harder to stop them once your puppy is an adult.

- Say no in a strong, confident voice whenever your Rottie starts chewing on anything that is not a toy or food or nips at you, another person, or another pet.

- Provide chew toys.

- Keep your Rottie in the puppy area until he no longer chews on furniture and items in reach.

- Get some puzzle toys to keep your Rottie's brain engaged (some chew out of boredom).

## Crate Training

*"As a breeder, I highly suggest crate training a new Rottweiler puppy. They will see this as their place to rest when needed and will help keep them safe from mischievous things they can get into."*

**Maria Bledsoe**
*JeMar Rottweilers*

Your Rottie's crate needs to be comfortable. Time in the crate is not meant to be a punishment, so you want your puppy to be comfortable. It should also be a part of the puppy area, with his bed. This gives him a safe space.

Crate training can help with housetraining as well. Rotties don't want to use the bathroom near their home – they don't want to soil their bedding. Having a pee pad in the puppy's area but as far from the crate as possible will help to make the point that it is to be used for bladder relief.

## Monitoring Aggression

Rottweilers are fiercely loyal and protective of their people, with a heavy emphasis on fierce if you don't train them from an early age. An untrained Rottweiler is a very serious potential danger. Working with your puppy to minimize any aggressive tendencies means taking training seriously and keeping an eye on your little companion.

One of the best ways to reduce potential aggression is to make sure your dog gets adequate exercise and playtime. Chapter 13 goes into detail about exercising your Rottie. This is one of the primary benefits of making sure your pup gets enough exercise – he will have a lot less energy left to get in trouble or to feel agitated. Training is not only good for helping your Rottie behave better, but it also helps to work out energy and keeps your pup mentally stimulated. Aggression can be a result of a lack of either mental or physical exercise. Training takes care of both problems.

# What Classes Can Offer To Help With Training Your Rottie

*"Rotties tend to gravitate to the one person who has the highest alpha status in the house. That's why it is important for all members of the household to get involved with a puppies training. Some Rotties will require an experienced dog trainer to teach both the humans and the puppy the basic fundamentals."*

**Deborah Brown**
*Black Jade Rottweilers*

It is strongly recommended that you enroll your Rottweiler in a training class. This has a dual purpose of helping you to socialize your Rottie while learning how to properly train him. This is the best environment for Rotties to learn how to socialize because dogs will be on their best behavior in a structured training class, and humans are more aware of their surroundings and their dog's behaviors. You will even get a chance to work on ensuring they don't try to dominate other dogs before they become adults. This will make it easier to take your buddy out for a jog, hiking, or other activities where there might be other dogs.

Individual trainers are best if you rescue a dog and you aren't sure how well socialized the dog is. It is easier for an adult to learn with a focused approach, especially if there has been little training up to this point in their life. However, for puppies, it is best to have classes, not keep them isolated with an individual trainer. If your rescue Rottie is also well socialized, it is best to enroll in a class.

CHAPTER 11.
# Basic Commands

*"The Rottweiler likes to please, but it is also a stubborn dog. You might give him a command and he will look at you thinking, 'do I really want to do this'. Be consistent, and do not give up or the Rottweiler will take over."*

**Grace Acosta**
*Acosta Rottweilers*

There is a good reason Rottweilers were the first guide dogs. This is a dog that is going to listen to you once you have their respect, and training will be a pleasure fairly quickly.

Once you get all of the basics down, plan to keep training. It may not be necessary, but tricks and different kinds of play can substitute for one (no more than that) of the at least 30-minute walks you need to take daily with your dog. During the winter or rainy days, this can be an absolute boon so that you don't freeze or get soaked. Your Rottie may not mind going outside, but you probably will. Having another option not only helps the two of you to bond, it can keep you more comfortable during inclement weather.

Photo Courtesy of
Debbie Bram
Flusstal Rottweilers

# Picking The Right Reward

One of the most interesting aspects of having a Rottie is determining the right reward. You want to keep the treats to a minimum but that should be fine with a Rottie since there are so many other things that can motivate them. Treats may be a good starting point, but you will need to quickly switch to something that is a secondary reinforcer. Praise, additional playtime, and extra petting are all fantastic rewards for Rotties since they care about how you feel and how you react to them. Plopping down to watch a movie and letting your puppy sit with you is a great reward after an intense training session. Not only did your puppy learn, but you both now get to relax and enjoy just chilling together.

If you begin to gain the respect of your Rottie, that can be used to help train your dog. At the end of each session, give your puppy extra attention or a nice walk to demonstrate how pleased you are with the progress that has been made.

# Successful Training

Photo Courtesy of
Clare Weston

Training is about learning commands. If your Rottie learns to respond only to rewards, the training was not successful.

Gaining the respect of your dog is generally the key in being a successful trainer, but with a Rottie it also means dedicated attention – you have all of the puppy's attention during a training session. As you and your Rottie work together, your dog will come to respect you (so long as you remain consistent and firm). Do not expect respect in the early days of training because your puppy doesn't understand the need for that yet. Fortunately, his intelligence will start to show early on and you can start switching to rewards that are fun instead of those that center around treats and food.

Even in the beginning, you need to make handling and petting a part of the reward. Although your dog does not quite understand it for what it is, your Rottie will begin to understand that treats and petting are both types of rewards. This will make it easier to switch from treats to a more attention-based reward system. Associating handling and petting as being enjoyable will also encourage your puppy to look at play time as a great reward. No matter how much they love to eat, being entertained and playing with you will be a welcome reward since it means the puppy is not alone or bored.

# Basic Commands

There are five basic commands that you must teach your Rottie. These commands are the basis for a happy and enjoyable relationship with your dog. By the time your puppy learns the five commands, the purpose of training will be clear to your Rottie. That will make it much easier to train him on the more complex concepts.

You should train the puppy in the specific order given below because each command builds from the next. Sit is a basic command, and something all dogs already do. Teaching leave it and how to bark less are both difficult and fight the instincts and desires of your Rottie pooch. These two commands will take longer to teach than the other commands, so you want to have the necessary tools already in place to increase your odds of success.

Here are some basic guidelines to follow during training.

- Everyone in the home should be a part of the Rottie training because the Rottie needs to learn to listen to everyone in the household, and not just one or two people. You may need to set a training schedule as training should involve only a couple of people. As mentioned in an earlier chapter, the puppy will need to learn to listen to everyone, so an adult should always be present, but including one child during training will help reinforce that the puppy listens to everyone in the house. It is also a good way for the parent to monitor the child's interaction so that everyone plays in a way that is safe and follows the rules.

**FUN FACT**
**ADRK**

The Allgemeiner Deutscher Rottweiler-Klub (ADRK) is the oldest club dedicated to the Rottweiler breed. Based in Minden/Westfalen in Germany, this club is recognized by the VDH in Germany as a dog-breeding club and aims to protect and preserve the Rottweiler breed. The club was founded in 1907.
Reference: https://adrk.de/index.php/en/verein/allgemeine-informationen

- To get started, select an area where you and your puppy have no distractions, including noise. Leave your phone and other devices out of range so that you keep your attention on the puppy.

- Stay happy and excited about the training. Your puppy will pick up on your enthusiasm, and will focus better because of it.

- Be consistent and firm as you teach.

- Bring a special treat to the first few training sessions, such as chicken or small treats.

## Sit

Photo Courtesy of Karace McLaughlin and Michael Palmertree

Start to teach *sit* when your puppy is around eight weeks old. Once you settle into your quiet training location with a special treat, begin the training.

**1.** Hold out the treat.

**2.** Move the treat over your puppy's head. This will make the puppy move back.

**3.** Say sit as the puppy's haunches touch the floor.

Having a second person around to demonstrate this with your puppy will be helpful as they can sit to show what you mean.

Wait until your puppy starts to sit down and say *sit* as he or she sits. If your puppy finishes sitting down, start to give praise for it. Naturally, this will make your puppy incredibly excited and wiggly, so it may take a bit of time before he or she will want to sit again. When the time comes and the puppy starts to sit again, repeat the process.

It's going to take more than a couple of sessions for the puppy to fully connect your words with the actions. In fact, it could take a little over a week for your puppy to get it. Commands are something completely new to your little companion.

Once your puppy has demonstrated a mastery over *sit,* it is time to start teaching *down.*

## Down

Repeat the same process to teach this command as you did for *sit*. Wait until the puppy starts to lie down, then say the word. If the Rottie finishes the action, offer your chosen reward.

It will probably take a little less time to teach this command.

Wait until your puppy has mastered *down* before moving on to *stay.*

## Stay

This command is going to be more difficult since it isn't something that your puppy does naturally. Be prepared for it to take a bit longer to train on this command. It is also important that your dog has mastered and will consistently sit and lie down on command before you start to teach *stay*. Stay can keep your puppy from running across a street or from running at someone who is nervous or scared of dogs.

Tell your puppy to either *sit* or *stay*. As you do this, place your hand in front of the puppy's face. Wait until the puppy stops trying to lick your hand before you begin again.

When the puppy settles

Photo Courtesy of Stacy Mendez

down, take a step away from the Rottweiler. If your puppy is not moving, say *stay* and give a treat and some praise for staying.

Giving the reward to your puppy indicates that the command is over, but you also need to indicate that the command is complete. The puppy has to learn to stay until you say it is okay to leave the spot. Once you give the okay to move, do not give treats. *Come* should not be used as the okay word as it is a command used for something else.

Repeat these steps, taking more steps further from the puppy after a successful command.

Once your puppy understands *stay* when you move away, start training to stay even if you are not moving. Extend the amount of time required for the puppy to *stay* in one spot so that he understands that *stay* ends with the okay command.

When you feel that your puppy has *stay* mastered, start to train the puppy to *come*.

## Come

This is a command you can't teach until the puppy has learned the previous commands. Before you start, decide if you want to use *come* or *come here* for the command. You will need to be consistent in the words you use.

This command is important for the same reason as the previous one. If you are around people who are nervous around dogs, or encounter a wild animal or other distraction, this command can snap your puppy's attention back to you.

Leash the puppy.

Tell the puppy to *stay*. Move away from the puppy.

Say the command you will use for *come* and give a gentle tug on the leash toward you. Repeat these steps, building a larger distance between you and the puppy. Once the puppy seems to get it, remove the leash and start at a close distance. If your puppy doesn't seem to understand the command, give some visual clues about what you want. For example, you can pat your leg or snap your fingers. As soon as your puppy comes running over to you, offer a reward.

## Leave It

This is going to be one of the most difficult commands you will teach your puppy because it goes against both your puppy's instincts and interests. Your puppy wants to keep whatever he has, so you are going to have to offer something better. It is essential to teach the command early though, as your Rottie is going to be very destructive in the early days. You want to get the trigger in place to convince the puppy to drop things. Furthermore this command could save your pooch's life. He is likely to lunge at things that look like food when you are out for a walk. This command gets him to drop any potentially hazardous meal.

You will need two different types of treats for this command. Since this is a more advanced basic command, you puppy will probably already be bored with one type of treat, or at least will be less enthusiastic about it. This will be your first treat. The newer, more interesting treat will be the reward treat.

1. Put one of each treat in each hand. If you want to use a clicker too, put it with the exciting treat.

2. Hide the less exciting treat, then hold it out to your puppy to let the little guy sniff your hand.

3. Say *Leave it*. Your puppy will keep sniffing, so you will need to wait until the sniffing stops (even if the treat is not exciting, it is still food).

4. When your puppy stops sniffing your hand, tell him or her *good* and hand over the exciting treat.

5. Repeat this immediately after your puppy finishes the exciting treat.

When your puppy stops sniffing as soon as you say leave it, you can graduate to the next phase.

1. Put the puppy's leash on.

2. Toss the less exciting treat out of reach.

3. Say *Leave it* and wait for the puppy to stop trying to get to the treat or trying to sniff in that direction.

4. When the puppy stops, tell him or her *good* and hand over the exciting treat.

You will need to keep reinforcing this command for months after it is learned because it is not a natural reaction. You can start to use your puppy's favorite toy in place of the less exciting treat. As the Rottie drops the toy, say *leave it*, and hand over the treat when the puppy shows that it will not go after the toy.

This is going to be one of those rare times when you must use a treat because your puppy needs something better to convince him or her to drop the toy. For now, your puppy needs that incentive, something more tempting than what he or she already has before your puppy can learn the command.

## Quiet

Even if Rottweilers aren't known for barking, that doesn't mean that they're all quiet. In the beginning, you can use treats sparingly to reinforce quiet if your pup enjoys making noise. If your puppy is barking for no apparent reason, tell the puppy to be quiet and place a treat nearby. It is almost guaranteed that the dog will fall silent to sniff the treat, in which case, say *good dog* or *good quiet*. It will not take too long for your puppy to understand that quiet means no barking.

# Where To Go From Here

The commands presented in this chapter are the foundation of training, and Rotties are capable of learning so much more. Just make sure that the tricks that you teach your Rottie are not too stressful for the puppy. As your puppy grows, you can start teaching tricks that highlight his agility. Fetch and other interactive tricks are ideal and fun.

If someone in your family suffers from an illness, including mental disorders like depression or autism, Rottweilers can be taught to help. Remember, there's a reason they were the first guide dogs. When properly trained, they can be incredibly productive family members that offer quiet support and a calming presence.

# CHAPTER 12.
# **Nutrition**

Rottweilers often make the lists of breeds most likely to become obese – a list that is largely dominated by small dogs. Rottweilers need to have their diet monitored, even when they are puppies. Not only do you have to be careful not to give your dog food from the "do not feed" list, but you must avoid food that is high in calories. As your pup gets older, this can become a serious issue. Ensuring your cute Rottie pup gets the right nutritional balance is critical for helping him a long, happy, healthy life.

Photo Courtesy of
Danielle Ingram

# Why A Healthy Diet Is Important

*"Rottweilers tend to have very sensitive stomachs. I recommend 4-5 star grain free foods (Earthborn, Merrick, Blue Wilderness and Royal Canin). Raw diets also work well."*

**Charles Robinson**
*Von Euro Kennel*

Many tricks and activities can expend a good bit of your Rottweiler's energy, but that doesn't mean that you can just let him eat whatever he wants. If you have a very busy schedule, it will be entirely too easy to have substantial lapses in activity levels while you are home. Your Rottweiler is still going to expect the same amount of food, regardless of activity level. This means he is likely to start putting on weight.

You need to be aware of roughly how many calories your dog eats a day including treats. If you notice that your dog is putting on weight, you will be able to adjust how much food the Rottweiler eats a day, or change the food to something with more nutritional value but fewer calories. Always talk with your vet if you have concerns about your Rottie's weight.

*Photo Courtesy of Tammy Bell*

# Commercial Food

Make sure that you are buying the best dog food that you can. Take the time to research each of your options, particularly the nutritional value of the food. Always account for your dog's size, energy levels, and age. Your puppy may not need puppy food as long as other breeds (or even other Rotties), and dog food for seniors may not be the best option for your senior Rottweiler. To provide more nutrition, you can mix some real food into the processed food. This can help supplement any nutrients, as well as being a healthy addition. The addition of a little bit of home-cooked food with each meal will make your Rottweiler excited to eat.

Pawster provides several great articles about which commercial dog foods are good for Rottweilers. Since new foods frequently come on the market, you will likely want to check back with them to see if there are newer, better foods once a year or every other year. Since you have to be careful of your Rottie's weight, it is well worth verifying that you are giving him some of the best foods for his needs.

If you aren't sure, talk with the breeder about what foods they recommend. You can ask your vet, but they are not usually Rottie specialists. This is one of the times where knowing what the breeders use will help keep your Rottie healthy.

# Preparing Your Food Naturally At Home

*"I feed a raw diet. Rottweilers do well on a diet higher in protein and fat. Puppies eat three times a day, and should be gaining anywhere from 8-12 lbs per month to ensure proper growth in the first year."*

**Deborah Bram**
*Flusstal Rottweilers*

If you regularly make your own food (from scratch, not with a microwave or boxed meal), it really doesn't take that much more time to provide an equally healthy meal for your companion.

Keeping in mind the foods that your Rottweiler absolutely should not eat, you can mix some of the food you make for yourself in your Rottweiler's meal. Just make sure to add a bit more of what your Rottweiler needs to the puppy food bowl. Although you and your Rottie have distinctly different dietary needs, you can tailor your foods to include nutrients that your dog needs. It won't really take that much longer to tailor a meal for you and a

Photo Courtesy of
Jade Skuse

*Photo Courtesy of
Abby Jane Veit*

slightly different version for your dog. Read through Chapter 4 to make sure that you never give your Rottweiler food that could be harmful or deadly.

Do not feed your Rottweiler from your plate. Split the food, placing your dog's meal into a bowl so that your canine understands that your food is just for you. The best home-cooked meals should be planned in advance so that your Rottweiler is getting the right nutritional balance.

Typically, 50% of your dog's food should be animal protein (fish, poultry, and organ meats). About 25% should be full of complex carbohydrates. The remaining 25% should be from fruits and vegetables, particularly foods like pumpkin, apples, bananas, and green beans. These provide additional flavor that your Rottweiler will probably love while making the little pup feel full faster so that the chance of overeating is reduced.

The following are a couple of sites you can use to make meals for Rotties (the sites are not Rottweiler specific, so if you have more than one dog, these meals can be made for all of your furry canine friends):

- K9 of Mine
- Dogsaholic

# Puppy Food Vs. People Food

It is true that puppies need more calories than adult dogs, but even with their size, Rottweiler puppies do not need nearly as much as you may think they do to meet caloric needs for their energy levels. If you are bringing a Rottweiler puppy into your home and know that you aren't going to have the time to cook, you should get food designed for puppies. This will ensure that your puppy gets the necessary calories for growth. Do not feed the puppy people food under the belief that you can switch to dog food later. Once your Rottweiler becomes an adult, it is nearly impossible to convince your canine that those unappetizing pellets are food, particularly when your dog knows what the food on your plate tastes like. Don't set a precedent that will create significant problems for yourself later. If you feed your Rottie home-cooked food, you are going to have to keep making food for your dog once the puppy stage is a memory.

Photo Courtesy of Stacy Schuckmann

# Weight Management

*"Don't let your Rottweiler get overweight. Bigger is definitely not better. Healthy and fit is most important."*

**Daviann Mitchell**
*Nighthawk Rottweilers*

It's important to maintain a regular eating schedule for your Rottie. His day is going to be based largely on mealtimes, and he will remind you if you feed him later usual. If treats and snacks are something you establish as normal early on, your dog is going to believe that is also a part of the routine and will expect them.

There needs to be a healthy balance of diet and exercise to keep your Rottweiler from becoming overweight. Exercise is an absolute must. While you are helping your Rottweiler develop healthy eating and exercise habits, you are probably helping yourself. Being more aware of your dog's diet and exercise levels will probably make you more aware of your own. Get used to exercising and playing as a reward system.

Weighing your Rottweiler will be helpful to ensure your pooch is staying at a healthy weight. Many vets allow you to weigh your pet for free. Stopping by every few months should be sufficient. If you see that your dog is gaining weight, find out what your vet recommends. Usually, they recommend reducing how much you give during the regular meals. While you should do this, it is likely extra food from treats and table scraps are the real reason why your dog is gaining weight. Take the time to understand what your Rottie is eating to keep his weight healthy.

## HELPFUL TIP
### A Stimulating Snack

Dogs are intelligent creatures and can become bored without adequate mental stimulation. The next time you want to give your dog a special treat, consider filling a rubber dog toy (be sure it's the appropriate size for your dog) with peanut butter or a mix of peanut butter and kibble. If you want to give your dog an extra challenge, consider freezing the toy before giving it to him or her. A note on peanut butter: do not give your dog peanut butter that contains xylitol or chocolate as both of these substances are harmful to dogs.

# CHAPTER 13.
# Exercising – Great Exercise Partners

If you love jogging or being outdoors, Rottweilers are an ideal companion for you. It is recommended that they get at least 2 hours of exercise a day. Inclement weather could present a challenge when you want to ensure your high-energy dog is getting what he needs in terms of activity, so this is why having a yard is best if you have a Rottie. Since Rottweilers want to please you, a long training session that expends energy means that you should occasionally be able to get away with just one or two walks on these days.

Photo Courtesy of
Alicia Copeland

# Exercise – Essential Need To Stay Active

*"Chasing a ball in the yard and nice log walks are both big in the Rottweiler world. Walking every day and a nice long game of fetch are usually sufficient for an adult Rottie."*

**Kathryn Lovan**
*Halo Rottweilers*

Rottweilers don't have an inordinate amount of energy – their energy levels are considered average – but they are large dogs. The amount of exercise they require is proportionate to their size, and that means you are going to be in for a good bit of walking, jogging, or playing every single day.

Remember, this is also a dog that is prone to being obese. This weight problem is directly a result of their need for a lot more exercise than what most people realize. When you think about a guard dog, you probably imagine a dog that sits around all day. They don't. And Rottweiler family dogs are just as active and enthusiastic as labs and golden retrievers – and as you will probably see fairly quickly they can be clowns when they are with family.

Because they are such intelligent dogs, you really don't want to let your dog get bored. Whether it's pulling dishes off countertops or eating couches, there is a lot of room for your large dog to do significant damage if he doesn't get enough exercise. One way to know when you have successfully tired out your Rottie is if he tries to curl up in your lap afterward to enjoy some petting and love.

Both for your Rottie's health and to keep the pup out of trouble, you have to make sure that your dog gets adequate exercise every day.

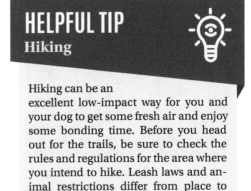

**HELPFUL TIP**
**Hiking**

Hiking can be an excellent low-impact way for you and your dog to get some fresh air and enjoy some bonding time. Before you head out for the trails, be sure to check the rules and regulations for the area where you intend to hike. Leash laws and animal restrictions differ from place to place. Also, be sure to check the weather and make sure you and your pup are properly attired for the forecast. Last but not least, pack plenty of water for both you and your dog!

# Leashing Training Essentials

*"A lot of exercise helps a Rottweiler to have an even temperament. Walk your dog, it helps the dog and the owner at the same time."*

**Charles Robinson**
*Von Euro Kennel*

Photo Courtesy of Liza Cadovius

Leash training isn't too difficult with a Rottie because they are such quick learners. Leash training begins pretty much from day one when you start housetraining your dog. You will need to start using this technique while walking your puppy during the first week. Even if you have a yard, your Rottie is going to be spending a considerable amount of time on the leash.

Once you have finished training your Rottie for all of the basic commands (Chapter 11), you should begin to teach your Rottie to heel. This is easily one of the hardest commands to teach, but it's one that you will need in order for your Rottie to be able to enjoy other kinds of leash activities. Given how powerful a Rottie is, you need to have control over him when you are out and about, which means making sure that your dog listens despite all of the distractions around you, starting from time he's a puppy. The best way to teach your puppy to heel is by learning from experts (this is why you need a class).

Heel is difficult to teach because it means a lot of stopping and waiting for your pup to listen to you. Only when you are certain that your pup is listening to you do you start walking again. Because of this, when you are teaching heel, it really doesn't count as exercise.

## Multiple Exercise Sessions

*"Exercise is good for everyone. As a puppy though, too much running/ jumping can cause issues. Their bones/joints are still growing and developing at such a young age. Do not allow any puppy to jump off of anything, and avoid steps until they are much older. A low impact exercise routine a few times a day is ideal."*

**Deborah Brown**
*`Black Jade Rottweilers*

With a recommendation of 2 hours of exercise every day, you know that you are going to be out exercising frequently. Neither you nor your Rottie is going to be happy trying to do a daily 2-hour stint, which means that you should plan to go outside to exercise several times a day.

Rotties are the ultimate motivator to get out and move. Those adorable eyes will convince you to get going, even if you don't really feel like doing it. This is the one time when giving in to those puppy-dog eyes is encouraged.

The schedule you have with a puppy will be very different. You definitely don't need to try for a full 2 hours with a puppy who is only a few months old. About 10 to 15 minutes at a time several times a day is enough, and as your pup ages, you can start making the play sessions longer.

# A Fantastic Jogging Companion

If you are looking for a great jogging companion, not many breeds are as perfect as the Rottweiler. However, you can't start jogging with your Rottweiler during the first year or two. Several considerations have to be met first.

- Large breed dogs should not go jogging until they are 18 months to 2 years old. Their bones require a longer wait before they're put through the difficulty of jogging since they weigh more than a small dog. Consult with your vet or a Rottweiler organizations on an appropriate starting age to start taking your Rottie jogging.

- It's best not to try to jog with your Rottie until you know that your dog understands the heel command.

- Your Rottie isn't wearing extra padding and protection on his or her feet, so as often as you can, jog on softer ground, such as dirt paths.

- Don't go for long runs in the beginning. Your Rottie needs build up stamina and understanding of what the activity is.

# Playtime! – Training For Rainy Or Hot Days

There will be days where it's either too hot or to0 rainy (or maybe even too snowy), but that won't stop your Rottweiler from being energetic. For those days, when you have to find alternatives to get rid of your Rottie's energy, consider the following. Keep in mind that you'll still need considerable space.

1. Use a laser pointer. While you can't play chase inside, your Rottie can chase the light of a laser pointer.

2. Tug of war is another great game that can help with other training as well. This is something you can start playing when your dog is a puppy, and it will also help him learn not to bite.

3. Hide and seek is a game you can play once your dog knows about proper behavior in the home. Since your Rottie will probably hear you wherever you hide, you can also make it a game of hide the toy. If you distract your pup while someone else hides the toy, your Rottie will have a good time trying to locate it.

4. Puzzle toys are a great way to get your dog to move around without you having to do much. Many of the games come with treats, and knowing Rottweilers, it won't be long before your dog figures out how to get the food out of the toy. Use these kinds of toys sparingly to avoid piling on the extra calories.

5. Rottweilers can learn to dance, sometimes even better than people. Occasionally, you can invite them up to dance on two legs, but you have

*Photo Courtesy of Sydney Masengarb*

*Photo Courtesy of Alexis Bynon*

to be very careful not to hurt them. It's best if you teach them how to dance while they're on all fours. That alone can tire you both out on a day when you can't go outside. Once your dog has the basics, start looking at some YouTube training videos on teaching your Rottie to dance. You can also look for trainers in your area, but if you and your Rottie are enrolled in classes, you should have all the tools you need by the time it is over to start training on your own. If you are interested, you could as your class instructor for recommendations on training or other classes to keep your Rottie socialized and learning.

## CHAPTER 14.
# Grooming – Productive Bonding

*"This is a very important part of owning a Rottweiler. From the day the owner brings home a puppy, I tell all my clients it's very important that they touch every part of their body, ears, feet, between toes, get into their mouth, their back end, this conditions the dog for 3 things, grooming, nail cutting and veterinarian care, it's important to have hands on with Rottweilers"*

**Deborah Bram**
*Flusstal Rottweilers*

Photo Courtesy of
Misty Ruggiero

Though your Rottie is short-haired, he's still a prolific shedder and therefore still requires regular grooming. Fortunately, this is fairly easy for Rotties as they aren't prone to problems with their coats. As long as you regularly brush your pup's teeth and monitor his eyes and ears to ensure they are healthy, Rotties are incredibly easy to groom.

Your Rottweiler's grooming needs include the following:

- Coat (bath and brushing)
- Eyes and ears
- Nails
- Teeth

# Grooming Tools

You don't need too many tools to properly groom your Rottie. Make sure you have the following on hand before your puppy or adult dog arrives:

- A bristle or pin brush for their coat
- Undercoat brush (this one is optional, but can help reduce shedding)
- Shampoo (check Pawster for the latest recommendations)
- Nail trimmers
- Toothbrush and toothpaste (check the American Kennel Club for the latest recommendations)

# Easy Coat Management

*"Rottweilers shed all year long and 'blow out' about twice a year. If you brush them daily they will shed less in your house. When you see they are shedding more than normal, you can do warm water baths and use a Furminator tool to pull the abundance of dead undercoat out quicker."*

**Teresa Bradley**
*Neu-Rodes Rottweilers*

While daily brushing is strongly recommended to keep the shedding down, if you start grooming when your puppy is young, it won't take you more than about 10 minutes once he is grown. This is fantastic considering how much time you will spend with other tasks, particularly exercise.

Photo Courtesy of
Zeta McCormack

## Puppy

When they are puppies, Rotties' coats aren't quite so coarse yet. Daily brushing not only can reduce how much your puppy sheds, but it helps you to build a bond with the puppy. Yes, it will be a bit challenging in the beginning because puppies don't sit still for long periods of time. There will be a lot of wiggling and attempts at play. Trying to tell your puppy that the brush is not a toy clearly isn't going to work, so be prepared to be patient during each brushing session. On the other hand, they are so adorable, you probably won't mind that it takes a bit longer. And this will be one of the only times when letting your pup sit in your lap won't put your legs to sleep (they will probably try to do it when they are older, so enjoy it while it lasts). Just make sure you let your pup know that this is a serious effort and playing comes after it. Otherwise, your Rottie is going to always try to play, which will make brushing him a lot more time consuming. Plan to brush your puppy after a vigorous exercise session so that your Rottweiler has far less energy to fight or play.

## Adulthood

Brushing daily is recommended because of how much they shed. If you properly train your puppy how to behave, this will be easy when he is an adult.

If you rescued an adult, it may take a little while to get the dog used to being brushed frequently. If you aren't able to get your dog to feel comfortable with the brushings in the beginning, you can work it into your schedule, like training. As your Rottie gets more comfortable, it will be easier to brush him or her daily.

# Cleaning Their Eyes And Ears

When you bathe your Rottweiler, you need to be careful not to get water in the ears. You should also make a habit of regularly checking not only his coat for sores or rashes but also his eyes and ears. He may have allergies that will make the inside of his ears that look red or reddish. If you see wax buildup, you can very gently wipe it away. Never put anything in your dog's ears though. A warm, moist pad can be used on the surface part of the ear. If it doesn't look better in a day, make an appointment to visit the vet.

Cataracts are a fairly common problem for all dogs as they age. You can generally tell if a dog has cataracts because they have a cloudy look. If you see cloudy eyes, have your Rottie checked to make sure he isn't developing cataracts. If he is, you many need to take the pup in to have them removed as cataracts can lead to blindness.

*Photo Courtesy of Kleper Souza*

# Bath Time

Given Rotties' size and short, dark coats, every few months should be more than enough to keep your pup clean, especially if you're brushing him daily. Set your bath schedule for about once a quarter (four times a year), and your puppy should be happy. Of course, if your Rottie gets dirty (which may happen whenever you go out exploring or hiking), then you'll need to take the time to bathe your canine.

Getting a dog this big into the bath really is not recommended. Look for a place where you can wash your dog nearby or in the yard. Of course, during the cold months, you can problem skip the baths entirely since you likely won't be out as much.

# Trimming The Nails

*"Keep their nails short, it is an ongoing job. I use a Dremel and diamond head to grind their nails. Be sure to start this very early so they are used to having their nails trimmed and do not protest too much."*

**Kathryn Lovan**
*Halo Rottweilers*

Rottweilers' toenails should not be long enough to click when they walk on hard floors or concrete. Cutting their nails is difficult because they're black like the dog's coat, which means that you may cut too much off and cause the quick to bleed. It's best to have an expert cut your dog's nails until you can see how it is done. If you do cut your Rottie's nails yourself, have some styptic powder near you in case you do cut too much.

To know when your pup needs those nails cut, pay attention to the sounds your dog makes when walking on harder surfaces to make sure that the nails aren't clicking. If they are, then you should increase how often you get his nails trimmed.

# Brushing Their Teeth

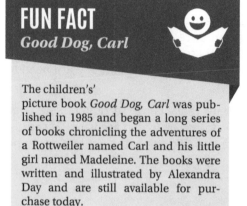

**FUN FACT**
*Good Dog, Carl*

The children's' picture book *Good Dog, Carl* was published in 1985 and began a long series of books chronicling the adventures of a Rottweiler named Carl and his little girl named Madeleine. The books were written and illustrated by Alexandra Day and are still available for purchase today.

Check with your vet to see what a good toothpaste is to use to brush your pup's teeth. Make sure to brush his teeth at least once a week to ensure he doesn't develop gum trouble. This is good practice for all dogs, so if you already have other canines, put them all on the same weekly brushing schedule.

If you aren't sure how to brush a dog's teeth, there are several tutorials online that you can use to get an idea of how to get around your Rottie's struggle to get away during the process. Like brushing the coat, Rottweilers need their teeth brushed often to avoid dental problems, and you probably will want to learn to do it yourself over having to visit a shop once a week. It's also nice to know how to do it if his breath smells bad or he ate something that smells foul.

You do need to get toothpaste made for dogs. Human toothpaste can upset their stomachs. The flavor of dog toothpaste will also make it easier to brush their teeth too – or at least entertaining as they try to eat it.

1. Put a little toothpaste on your finger and hold it out to your dog.

2. Let your dog lick the toothpaste.

3. Praise your dog for trying something new.

4. Put a little toothpaste on your finger, lift up your dog's upper lip, and begin to rub in circles along your Rottie's gums. Your pup will very likely make it difficult by constantly trying to lick your finger. Give your puppy praise when he or she doesn't wiggle too much.

   a. Try to move in a circular motion. This will be very tricky, especially with those sharp baby teeth.

   b. Try to keep the puppy still without putting the little pooch in a vise grip. As your puppy gets bigger, you need him or her to sit for the cleaning voluntarily.

   c. Try to massage both the top and bottom gums. It is likely that the first few times you won't be able to do much more than get your finger in your dog's mouth, and that's okay. Over time, your puppy will learn to listen as training elsewhere helps your dog understand when you are giving commands.

5. Stay positive. No, you probably won't be able to clean the puppy's teeth for a while, and that is perfectly fine. Training a child to brush their teeth takes longer, so know that at some point it won't be so bad.

Once your dog seems all right with you brushing with your finger, try the same steps with a toothbrush. It may be a similar song and dance in the beginning, but it shouldn't take nearly so long. It could take a couple of weeks before you can graduate to a toothbrush, but even if it does take that long, it is still great bonding time.

## CHAPTER 15.
# Health Issues

This chapter covers basic health care for any dog (Rottie-specific issues are covered in the next chapter). For the most part, these are environmental issues, so your concerns will vary based on where you live. For example, if you live near woods, your dog is at a greater risk of ticks than a dog that lives in the city. Talk to your vet about risks to your dog.

If you have more than one dog, these are things you should be doing for all of them. You can consider this chapter as more of a reminder or checklist of things you probably already know you need to be aware of.

If you have never had a dog before, bookmark this chapter because there is a lot of information to take in – dogs require just as much attention to their health as humans. Most of this chapter covers basic preventative measures you should take to make sure your puppy or adult dog stays healthy.

Photo Courtesy of Amanda Pittigher

# Fleas And Ticks

Given how much Rotties love the outdoors, they're at a much greater risk of both ticks and fleas than other dogs, and neither are easy to see because of that dark coat. Therefore, you can't allow any lapse in treatment, even in winter.

Make it a habit to check for ticks after every outing into the woods, long grass, or near wild plants. Comb through the fur and check the skin for irritation and parasites. Since you will be

doing this often, you should be able to tell when a bump is a problem. Since your dog will be very happy to spend time with you, it shouldn't take as long as you might think – it isn't as though you'll have to spend a lot of time struggling to get your Rottie to sit still for a tick check.

Fleas will be more problematic because they're far more mobile. The best way to look for fleas is to make it a regular part of your brushing sessions. You can also look for behavioral indicators, such as incessant scratching and licking. With the regular checks on your pup's skin when you are brushing his or her fur, you will be able to check the spots where your dog is scratching to see if the skin is irritated or if it is the work of a flea. You will need to use flea preventative products on a regular basis once your puppy reaches an appropriate age. Make sure to read the packaging to find out when is right to begin treating your dog based on the current age and size. Different brands have different recommendations, and you do not want to start treating your puppy too early. There are also very important steps for to apply the treatment. Make sure you understand all of this before you purchase the flea treatment.

If you want to use natural products instead of chemical ones, set aside a few hours to research the alternatives and find out what works best for your Rottie. Don't increase the number of baths – that isn't a good solution. Verify that any natural products work before you buy them and make sure you consult with your vet. Establishing a regular schedule and adding it to the calendar will help you remember to treat your dog each month.

*Photo Courtesy of Bobbi Lambier*

Rottweilers with allergies may develop hot spots that you think are fleas initially. Hot spots are inflamed areas of the skin that when left untreated can result in fur loss or a lot of itching. If you notice your dog scratching and can't find evidence of fleas, it could actually be an allergic reaction. Take your Rottie to the vet if you notice a lot of scratching but aren't sure of the reason.

# Worms And Parasites

Although worms and other types of parasites are a less common problem than fleas and ticks, they can be far more dangerous. There are a number of types of worms that you should be aware of:

- Heartworms
- Hookworms
- Roundworms
- Tapeworms
- Whipworms

One of the primary problems is that there isn't an easy to recognize set of symptoms to help identify when your dog has a problem with worms. However, you can keep an eye out for these symptoms, and if your dog shows them, you should schedule a visit to the vet.

- If your Rottweiler is unexpectedly lethargic for at least a few days.
- Patches of fur begin to fall out (this will be noticeable if you brush your Rottweiler regularly) or if you notice patchy spaces in your dog's coat. It could be allergies. But whatever the reason, fur falling out is never a good thing.
- If your dog's stomach becomes distended (expands) and looks like a potbelly, set up a vet appointment immediately to have him or her checked for worms.
- Your Rottweiler begins coughing, vomiting, has diarrhea, or has a loss in appetite.

These symptoms should be more obvious in a Rottie because they tend to be active or with you all of the time. If you aren't sure, it is best to get to the vet as soon as possible to check.

If your dog has hookworms or roundworms, you will also need to visit a doctor to get checked. These worms can be spread to you from your dog through skin contact. If your dog has them, you are at risk of contracting them. Being treated at the same time as your Rottie can help stop the vicious cycle of continually switching which of you has worms.

Heartworms are a significant threat to your dog's health and can be deadly as they slow and stop blood flood. You should be actively treating your dog to ensure that this parasite does not have a home in your dog. There are medications that can ensure your Rottie does not get or have heartworms.

# Benefits Of Veterinarians

From vaccines to health checkups, regularly scheduled vet visits will make sure that your Rottie stays healthy. Since Rotties are such eager companions, it will be obvious when they aren't acting the way they normally do. You will notice the changes, especially if your Rottweiler stops following you around the house. Annual visits to the vet will ensure there isn't a problem that is slowly draining the energy or health from your dog.

Photo Courtesy of Destiny Evans

Health checkups also make sure that your Rottie is aging well. If there are any early symptoms of something potentially wrong with your dog over the years (such as arthritis), you will be able to start making adjustments. The vet can help you come up with ways to manage pain and problems that come with the aging process and will be able to recommend adjustments to the schedule to accommodate your canine's aging body and diminishing abilities. This will ensure that you can keep having fun together without hurting your dog.

# Holistic Alternatives

Wanting to keep a dog from a lot of exposure to chemical treatments makes sense, and there are many good reasons why people are moving to more holistic methods. However, doing this does require a lot more research and monitoring to ensure that the methods are working – and more importantly, do not harm your dog. Unverified holistic medicines can be a waste of money, or, worse, they can even be harmful to your pet. However, natural methods that work are always preferable to any chemical solution.

Photo Courtesy of Francisco Bustamante

If you decide to go with holistic medication, talk with your vet about your options. You can also seek out Rottie experts to see what they recommend before you start using any methods you are interested in trying. Read what scientists have said about the medicine you are considering. There is a chance that the products you buy from a store are actually better than some holistic medications.

Make sure you are thorough in your research and that you don't take any unnecessary risks with the health of your Rottie.

# Vaccinating Your Rottweiler

Vaccination schedules are almost universal for all dog breeds, including Rottweilers. The following list can help you ensure your Rottie receives the necessary shots on schedule. Make sure to add this to your calendar

- The first shots are required between 6 and 8 weeks of age. You should find out from the breeder if these shots have been taken care of and get the records of the shots:
  - Corona virus
  - Distemper
  - Hepatitis
  - Leptospirosis
  - Parainfluenza
  - Parvo
- These same shots are required again between 10 and 12 weeks of age.
- These same shots are required again between 14 and 15 weeks of age, as well as the first rabies shot.
- Your dog will need to get these shots annually for his whole life.

# CHAPTER 16.
# Health Concerns

*"Rottweilers are very susceptible to cancer and the chances of cancer exponentially increase if a dog is spayed or neutered under a year of age. Delay the sterilization process as long as possible."*

**Daviann Mitchell**
*Nighthawk Rottweilers*

**Photo Courtesy of Cheyenne Simpson**

All pure breed dogs have known genetic issues. Breeders now actively work to ensure these kinds of problems are not perpetuated as much as possible, but you still have to be aware of the potential problems because there is no guarantee that your canine won't have some of the genetic issues. Good breeders offer guarantees to ensure their puppies can be returned if they have one of a particular breed's known genetic issues. To meet the requirements of these guarantees you have to know the problems and their symptoms. The sooner you start to counter any potential problems, the healthier your Rottie is likely to be.

Adopting a puppy can give you the span of a dog's entire life to ensure your dog is as healthy as possible. The breeder should be able to provide health records in addition to any shot records and required tests. All of the details on the genetic and common ailments of Rottweilers are in Chapter 3. Making sure that the parents are healthy increases the likelihood that your puppy will remain healthy over his or her entire life. However, there is still a chance that your dog will have one of these documented problems even if the parents don't, so you will still need to keep an eye on your friend.

Large breeds have their own set of problems because the size is hard on the larger dogs' bodies.

# A Long Breed History Means A Longer List Of Potential Health Problems

Rottweilers have the same kinds of problems that most large dogs have. Those larger bodies simply don't age as slowly as the smaller dogs. There are two primary problems that you need to watch for with your Rottie.

## Hips, Joints, And Ligaments

*"Hips tend to be the biggest health issue with Rottweilers. I recommend only buying puppies with OFA GOOD parents. There is also the European Hip grade A or B that are acceptable."*

**Charles Robinson**
*Von Euro Kennel*

Hip and elbow dysplasia is far more noticeable early in larger breeds. The different types of dysplasia mean that the joints don't correctly fit into the sockets. This affects the back half of a dog's body first, and it is a real problem that your Rottie may try to hide. Your pup will walk a little more stiffly, or may pant even when it's not hot.

You will need to keep an eye on your dog's hind quarters because things like hip and elbow dysplasia are a lot more obvious in large dogs because their movements appear to be more exaggerated. Watch your dog for signs of this and adjust your exercise so that you and your Rottie aren't going too far on your walks. Do tricks and other indoor activities that are easier on their back half.

Photo Courtesy of Courtney Marshbank

You also need to watch for cruciate ligament rupture. This condition can be incredibly painful for your dog and manifests itself in limping or lameness. It likely will require surgery. It can be hereditary, but size can cause this problem too. This is another reason why you need to make sure your Rottie stays in a healthy weight range.

## Body

Aortic Stenosis is a heart condition that obstructs a dog's blood flow. This is a genetic Rottie disease, so it should be a condition that is covered by the guarantee. Your Rottie's long back makes him more prone to back injuries too, so this is why you have to be careful and avoid lifting your Rottie as he or she ages.

# Typical Pure-Breed Health Issues

The different types of dysplasia and arthritis are the biggest issues, and these are the ones that you really need to watch for.

## Where You Can Go Wrong

In addition to genetic problems, there are things that you can do that could damage your dog's health related to diet and exercise levels. If you follow the recommendations in Chapter 15, your dog will remain healthy longer. In addition to these problems already listed, the following are some of the potential issues you would be aware of and watch for signs of:

- Entropion – the dog's eyelids roll inward, damaging the cornea.
- Ectropion – the dog's eyelids roll outward; typically a condition in puppies that may go away by adulthood.
- Juvenile Laryngeal Paralysis & Polyneuropathy – a genetic disease that affects a dog's nerves. Usually it starts with the voice box, and then starts to affect other areas.

- Wet eczema – common to most breeds with such thick coats, the skin can become irritated very quickly.

## Importance Of Breeder To Ensuring Health In Your Rottweiler

Any breeder who doesn't provide a health guarantee for a breed as established as the Rottweiler is not a breeder you should consider getting a dog from. Avoid all of these breeders – they are interested in the money, and the dog's health is of little to no concern. If

Photo Courtesy of Kristoffer Larsson

a breeder says that a puppy or litter has to be kept in an isolated location for health reasons, don't work with that breeder.

Ask the breeder to talk about the history of the parents, the kinds of health problems that have been in the dog's family, and if the breeder has had problems with any particular illnesses in the past. If the breeder gives you only short or vague answers, this is a sign that the breeder has dogs that are more likely to have issues later.

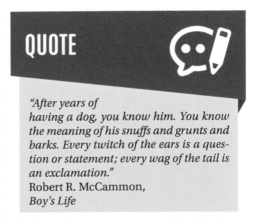

**QUOTE**

*"After years of having a dog, you know him. You know the meaning of his snuffs and grunts and barks. Every twitch of the ears is a question or statement; every wag of the tail is an exclamation."*
Robert R. McCammon,
*Boy's Life*

# Prevention & Monitoring

Always pay attention to your Rottie's weight. With hip and elbow dysplasia being a real genetic problem, additional weight will only worsen things. Your vet will likely talk to you if your dog is overweight because this not only puts a strain on the dog's legs, joints, and muscles, but it can also have adverse effects on your dog's heart, blood flow, and respiratory system. Make sure to talk to your vet if you notice that your Rottie is having any trouble. Those regular vet visits can help you address issues that you may not think are that big a deal. Sometimes the symptoms you notice are a sign of a future problem.

Photo Courtesy of
Cassi Naden

# CHAPTER 17.
# **Your Aging Rottweiler**

While smaller breeds aren't considered seniors until usually around 9, Rottweilers (and most large dogs) are considered seniors at 7.5 years old. As your dog ages, you will need to start making adjustments to accommodate his or her reduced abilities. A dog may remain healthy his or her entire life, but his body still won't be able to do the same activities at 8 years that it could do at 2. The changes you make will be based on your Rottie's specific needs. With larger dogs, the decline seems to happen a lot faster, almost suddenly. The thing is that the signs are there, but we really don't want to see them.

If you jog with your Rottie, you will need to stop once you notice the signs. Your Rottie will get tired sooner. He may walk a little stiffer. Start to tone back the jogs, or stop and just go for more energetic walks.

As your Rottie's energy and abilities decrease, you need to make sure that he isn't overdoing it. You should always make sure your dog doesn't over exercise, but this is even more important for an older dog. Rotties may be too focused on having fun to realize they're hurting until they stop to rest. It's easy to make the senior years incredibly enjoyable for your Rottie and yourself by making the necessary adjustments that allow your dog to keep being active without overexertion.

*Photo Courtesy of Jason Parnis*

# Senior Dog Care

It's usually easier to take care of a senior dog than a young dog, and Rotties are no exception. Naps are just as exciting as walks. Sleeping beside you while you watch television or as you yourself nap is pretty much all it takes to make your Rottie happy.

*Photo Courtesy of Denice Pare*

However, you must continue to be vigilant about diet and exercise. Now is not the time to let your Rottie start to eat anything and everything or neglect to take your regular walks.

If your canine can't manage long walks, make the walks shorter and more numerous and spend more time romping around your yard or home.

When it comes to items that your Rottie will need to access regularly, you should:

- Set water bowls out in a couple of different places so that your dog can easily reach them as needed. If your Rottweiler shows signs of having trouble drinking or eating, place slightly raised water dishes around the home to make it easier for him.

- Cover hard floor surfaces (such as tiles, hardwood, and vinyl). Use non-slip carpets or rugs.

- Add cushions and softer bedding for your Rottie. This will both make the surface more comfortable and help your Rottie stay warmer. There are bed warmers for dogs if your Rottie displays achy joints or muscles often. Of course, you also need to make sure your Rottie isn't too warm, so this can be a fine balancing act.

Photo Courtesy of
Lisa Steeves

- To improve his or her circulation, increase how often you brush your Rottie. This should be very agreeable to your Rottie as a way to make up for other limitations that mean you must do other activities less often.

- Stay inside in extreme heat and cold. Your Rottie is hardy, but the old canine body cannot handle the extreme changes as well as once it did.

- Use stairs or ramps for your Rottie wherever possible so that the old pup doesn't have to try to jump.

- Avoid moving your furniture around, particularly if your Rottie shows signs of having trouble with his sight. A familiar home is more comforting and less stressful as your pet ages. If your Rottie isn't able to see as clearly as he once did, keeping the home familiar will make it easier for your dog to move around without getting hurt.

- If you have stairs, consider setting up an area where your dog can stay without having to go up and down too often.

- Create a space where your Rottie can relax with fewer distractions and noises. Don't make your old friend feel isolated, but do give him or her a place to get away from everyone if he needs to be alone.

- Be prepared to let your dog out more often for restroom breaks.

# Nutrition

Since a decrease in exercise is inevitable for any aging dog, you will need to adjust your pet's diet. If you opt to feed your Rottie commercial dog food, make sure you change to a senior food. If you make your Rottie's food, take the time to research how best to reduce calories without sacrificing taste and talk to your vet. Your canine is going to need less fat in his food, so you may need to find something healthier that still has a lot taste to supplement the types of foods you gave your Rottie as a puppy or active adult dog.

# Exercise

Exercise will be entirely up to you because your Rottie is still just happy to be with you. If you make fewer demands, decrease the number of walks, or in any way change the routine, your Rottie will quickly adapt to the new program. It's up to you to adjust the schedule and keep your Rottweiler happily active. Usually increasing the number of walks with shorter durations will help keep your Rottie as active as necessary.

The way your Rottie slows down will probably be the hardest part of watching him age. You will probably notice that your Rottie spends more time sniffing. This could be a sign that your dog is tiring, or it could be his way of acknowledging that long steady walks are a thing of the past and so he is stopping to enjoy the little things more. Your Rottie may also let you know that it is time to go home by turning around to go back or sitting down a lot and looking at you. Take the hint and go home if your Rottie lets you know that the limits have been reached.

# Mental Stimulation

Unlike the body, your Rottweiler's mind is likely to be just as sharp and clever in the golden years. That means you should start making adjustments to focus more on activities that are mentally stimulating. Once your Rottie understands the basics, you can start doing training for fun because your Rottie will be just as able to learn now as when he or she was 1 year old. Actually, it is likely to be easier be-

*Photo Courtesy of Heleen Schilleman*

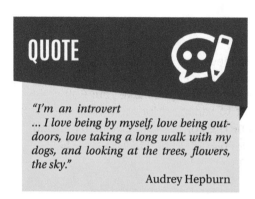

**QUOTE**

*"I'm an introvert ... I love being by myself, love being outdoors, love taking a long walk with my dogs, and looking at the trees, flowers, the sky."*

Audrey Hepburn

cause your Rottie has learned to focus better and he'll be happy to have something he can still do with you.

Getting your senior Rottweiler new toys is one way to help keep your dog's mind active if you don't want to train your dog again or if you just don't have the time. Whatever toys you get, make sure they aren't too rough on your dog's older jaw and teeth. Tug of war may be a game of the past (you don't want to hurt the old teeth), but other games such as hide and seek are still very much appreciated. Whether you hide toys or yourself, this can be a game that keeps your Rottie guessing.

## Regular Vet Exams

Just as humans go to visit the doctor more often as they age, you'll need to take your dog to see your vet with greater frequency. The vet can make sure that your Rottie is staying active without overdoing it, and that there is no unnecessary stress on your older dog. If your canine has sustained an injury and hidden it from you, your vet is more likely to detect it.

Your vet can also make recommendations about activities and changes to your schedule based on your Rottweiler's physical abilities and any changes in personality. For example, if your Rottie is panting more now, it could be a sign of pain from stiffness. This could be difficult to distinguish given how much Rotties pant as a rule, but if you see other signs of pain, schedule a visit with the vet. Your vet can help you determine the best way to keep your Rottie happy and active during the later years.

## Common Old-Age Ailments

Chapters 4 and 16 cover illnesses that are common or likely with a Rottweiler, but old age tends to bring a slew of ailments that aren't particular to any one breed. Here are the things you will need to watch for (as well as talking to your vet about them).

- Diabetes is probably the greatest concern for a breed that loves to eat as much as your Rottie does, even with 2 hours of daily exercise most of the dog's adult life. Once they are old, Rotties need less food because they won't be able to exercise nearly as much. Although it is usually thought of as a genetic condition, any Rottie can become diabetic if not fed and exercised properly. This is another reason why it's so important to be careful with your Rottie's diet and exercise levels.

- Arthritis is probably the most common ailment in any dog breed, and the Rottie is no exception. If your dog is showing signs of stiffness and pain after normal activities, talk with your vet about safe ways to help minimize the pain and discomfort of this common joint ailment.

- Gum disease is a common issue in older dogs as well, and you should be just as vigilant about brushing teeth when your dog gets older as you were at any other age. A regular check of your Rottie's teeth and gums can help ensure this does not become a problem.

- Loss of eyesight or blindness is relatively common in older dogs, just as it is in humans. Unlike humans, however, dogs don't do well with wearing glasses. Have your dog's vision checked at least once a year and more often if it is obvious that his eyesight is failing.

- Kidney disease is a common problem in older dogs, and one that you should monitor for the older your Rottie gets. If your canine is drinking more often and having accidents regularly, this could be a sign of something more serious than just aging. If you notice this happening, get your Rottie to the vet as soon as possible and have him or her checked for kidney disease.

# Enjoying The Final Years

The last years of your Rottie's life can be just as enjoyable (if not more so) than the earlier stages. The energy and activities that the two of you used to do will be replaced with more attention and relaxation than at any other time. Finally having your Rottie be calm enough to just sit still and enjoy your company can be incredibly nice (just remember to keep up his activity levels instead of getting too complacent with your Rottie's newfound love of resting and relaxing).

*Photo Courtesy of Rachel Labidi*

## Steps And Ramps

Rotties are large, so you should never try to lift them up to put them in a vehicle or anything else. Picking up your dog more often can do even more physical harm. Steps and ramps are the best way to ensure your Rottie can maintain some level of self-sufficiency as he ages. Also, using steps and ramps provides a bit of different activity that can work as a way of getting a bit of extra exercise.

## Enjoy The Advantages

A Rottie can be just as much fun in old age because his or her favorite thing is being with you, especially if you do the extra training for mental tricks such as asking him to learn the names of new toys and having him then bring them to you. Your pet is just as enthusiastic as during the early years, but has learned to chill a bit more.

Your older pet will find the warmest and most comfortable places, and will want you to join him. Your dog is incredibly devoted and will be happy to just share a short stroll followed by a lazy evening at home. You should keep the same number of walks, but make them shorter based on how your Rottie is doing.

## What To Expect

Photo Courtesy of
Tonya Renee Jones
Lakeview Kennel

Your Rottweiler probably isn't going to suffer from fear that you are less interested in spending time together. He or she will continue be a loving companion, interacting with you at every opportunity – that does not change with age. Just how much they can do changes. Your canine's limitations should dictate interactions and activities. If you are busy, make sure you schedule time with your Rottie to do things that are within those limitations. Your happiness is still of utmost importance to your dog, so let the old companion know you feel the same way about his or her happiness. It is just as easy to make an older Rottweiler happy as it is with a young one, and it is easier on you since relaxing is more essential to your old friend.

## Vet Visits

As your Rottie ages, you are going to notice the slow-down, and the pains in your Rottie's body are going to be obvious just like in an older person. You need to make sure that you have regular visits with your vet to make sure that you aren't doing anything that could potentially harm your Rottie. If your Rottweiler has a debilitating ailment or condition, you may want to discuss the options for ensuring a better quality of life, such as wheels if your Rottie's legs begin to have serious issues. In the worst cases, you may want to discuss the quality of your Rottweiler's life with the vet.

CPSIA information can be obtained
at www.ICGtesting.com
Printed in the USA
BVHW091533160920
588927BV00001B/14